# MATHEMATICS

*A Curriculum Development Study*
based on
The Low Attainers in Mathematics Project

**carried out at**
**The Mathematics Centre, West Sussex Institute of Higher Education**

in conjunction with
Dorset, East Sussex, Hampshire, Isle of Wight, Surrey and West Sussex
Local Education Authorities

Project Director: Afzal Ahmed

London: Her Majesty's Stationery Office

# Contents

# PREFACE

The Low Attainers in Mathematics Project (LAMP) was one of three post-Cockcroft Department of Education and Science (DES) studies related to low attainers. The Project was based at the Mathematics Centre, West Sussex Institute of Higher Education (WSIHE). The funding bodies were the DES, the Local Education Authorities of Dorset, East Sussex, Hampshire, Isle of Wight, Surrey and West Sussex, and WSIHE.

## SECTION A — PROJECT PERSONNEL

Director: Afzal Ahmed
Project Secretary: Jean Dann

**Teacher–researchers** The following classroom teachers were released by their Local Education Authorities for one day a week for three years to work both at WSIHE and in schools.

| | | |
|---|---|---|
| DORSET | St. Edwards R.C. School, Poole. (12–16) | Bernadette Cherowbrier |
| | The Grange School, Christchurch. (11–16) | Gill Snook<br>Head of Remedial Department. |
| EAST SUSSEX | Tideway School, Newhaven. (11–18) | Frankie Sulke<br>(released for 2 days a week) |
| HAMPSHIRE | Bohunt School, Liphook. (11–16) | Terry Bevis<br>Head of Mathematics Department. |
| | St. Vincent School, Gosport. (11–16) | Cherry Edwards<br>Head of Mathematics Department. |
| | City of Portsmouth Boys' School, Portsmouth. (11–18) | Dianne Harmer (until Dec. 1984)<br>Head of Mathematics Department.<br>Richard Goman (from Jan. 1985)<br>Head of Mathematics Department. |
| ISLE OF WIGHT | Kitbridge Middle School, Newport. (9–13) | Mary Brading<br>Mathematics Coordinator. |
| | Ryde High School, Ryde. (13–18) | Chris Tagart |
| SURREY | De Burgh School, Burgh Heath. (12–18) | Linda Finn |
| | Wayneflete School, Esher. (12–16) | Honor Williams<br>Head of Mathematics Department. |
| WEST SUSSEX | Downsbrook Middle School, Worthing. (7–12) | Peter Greenland (until July 1985)<br>Second Master.<br>Sian Howie (from Sept. 1985) |
| | St. Andrew's (C.E.) Boys' School, Worthing. (12–16) | Tas Smith (until July 1985)<br>Tony Eden (from Sept. 1985) |

| **WSIHE Mathematics Centre Staff** | John Mitchell | Head of Mathematics Section. |
| | Pam Bartlett | Teacher–fellow 1984–6 seconded from Birmingham Mathematics Centre. |
| | Adrian Pinel | |
| | Simon Relf | |
| | Marion Bird | As a consultant. |
| | Adrian Oldknow | As a consultant. |
| | Nigel Bufton | As a consultant. |

| **Steering Committee** | Professor Brian Griffiths (Chairman) | University of Southampton, Department of Mathematics. |
| | Nick Sanders (until April 1986) | Assistant Secretary, DES. |
| | Monty Capey (from May 1986) | Assistant Secretary, DES. |
| | Arnold Ashbrook (until April 1986) | HMI Staff Inspector, Mathematics. |
| | Jim Mayhew (from May 1986) | HMI Staff Inspector, Mathematics. |
| | Afzal Ahmed | Director, Low Attainers in Mathematics Project, WSIHE. |
| | John Backhouse | University of Oxford, Department of Educational Studies. |
| | Derek Foxman | NFER Principal Research Officer. |
| | Enid Layson | Mathematics Adviser, East Sussex. |
| | Henry Macintosh | Secretary, Southern Regional Examinations Board. |
| | Ray Peacock | Divisional Manager, Mullard Mitcham. |
| | Michael Pipes | Headmaster, City of Portsmouth Boys' School. |
| | Roy Potter | Director of Education, West Sussex. |
| | Gerry Price | Mathematics Adviser, Hertfordshire. |
| | John Wyatt | Director, WSIHE. |

The Committee met on 10 occasions. Some teacher–researchers and WSIHE staff attended each meeting.

| **Management Committee** | Afzal Ahmed | Director, Low Attainers in Mathematics Project, WSIHE. |
| | Bob Cory | Mathematics Adviser, Dorset. |
| | Frank Gregory | Mathematics Adviser, Isle of Wight. |
| | Alan Kaye | General Inspector for Mathematics, Surrey. |
| | Enid Layson | Mathematics Adviser, East Sussex. |
| | John Mitchell | Head of Mathematics Section, WSIHE. |
| | Judy Morgan (until Dec. 1985) | Mathematics Adviser, West Sussex. |
| | Dianne Harmer (from Jan. 1985) | Mathematics Adviser, West Sussex. |
| | Derek Pitman | Mathematics Adviser, Hampshire. |

The Committee met on 18 occasions.

*NB. All designations are those that applied at the commencement of the Project in September 1983.*

The Project aimed to develop and encourage 'good practice' in mathematics teaching. Its work is ongoing. The development is now taking place in the classrooms of some 2000 teachers throughout the six authorities with pupils across the age and ability range. The teachers are part of a continually growing and developing network of working groups. The work undertaken by teachers involved in the Project network has deliberately focused on improving pupils' achievement, attitudes, confidence and interest in mathematics. Within the network are approximately 200 teachers who, over the period of the Project, have been released from their teaching commitments on one day a week for a year (on various Mathematical Association diploma courses based at WSIHE). This time has enabled these teachers to engage in even greater reflection, experimentation and evaluation of their own classroom practice. This research is supported by substantial 'case study' writing produced by each of them over a period of two years. The Project also has an extensive stock of writing arising from the active involvement of teachers (at all levels including senior management), pupils, advisory staff, parents, employers and college staff involved in initial and in-service provision.

The nature of the report reflects the quality of all this ongoing personal classroom-based research. The recommendations for action and the statements made are careful distillations of these experiences. The report is hence an invitation to those concerned with education at *all* levels to experiment, discuss, debate, strengthen and refute as a result of their *own* experiences. It is about taking action.

# 1

# INTRODUCTION

*"It's all been said before. Why don't things change?"*

*"Why do so many published projects have such a short life, whereas some textbooks go on forever?"*

*"Why can children handle money situations in town on Saturday and fail to do the 'sums' in school on Monday?"*

*"It's all right in theory, but it couldn't happen in my school."*

*"There are plenty of ideas and resources around. Why are they so little used?"*

*"Why doesn't educational research help children more in the classroom?"*

*"Why do 'ordinary' teachers who start to work together immediately become reclassified as 'special' teachers?"*

*"How does a child get to the state of wailing, 'But I can't do fractions Miss!', as soon as the title is put on the board?"*

*"Yes, but what about: the syllabus . . . my Head . . . examinations . . . parents . . . employers . . . under-qualified teachers . . . probationers . . . my head of department . . . lack of resources . . . large classes . . .?" . . . add your own.*

Questions and remarks of this kind surface as soon as issues relating to mathematics teaching and learning are discussed, and it is therefore not surprising that these issues have been central concerns in the Project's work.

*Details of the background, initial aims and specific outcomes of the Project can be found in the Project Review (page 85).*

The Project, a follow-up to the Cockcroft enquiry, was charged in the first instance with the task of developing and encouraging 'good practice' in the teaching of mathematics to low attaining pupils and then to investigate methods of disseminating its findings. It became clear to us at an early stage that low attainment was not only a problem for pupils in the 'bottom 40%' attainment range. For example, many teachers express concern that their sixth formers do not fulfil their potential in the subject in terms of their ability to transfer and apply mathematics. Teachers involved in the Project have written about the relevance of the work they are doing in their classrooms to all the pupils they teach. They found the changes they were making in their teaching approaches were encouraging *all* their pupils to become more involved in their mathematics and to surpass traditional expectations at every level. The problem became one of under-achievement across the whole age and ability range.

Specific concerns such as the problem of girls and mathematics, and the use of computers in mathematics, important as they are, did not emerge as different in essence from the Project's general concern to improve the quality of pupils' mathematics. Society's attitudes play a large part in conditioning girls' feelings towards the subject, and these attitudes may condition a teacher's expectations. This is of major concern. Nevertheless, the problems of motivation, sustaining girls' interest and raising their level of attainment in mathematics classrooms involve the same strategies as for *all* pupils. Computers have brought a wealth of new possibilities to the mathematics classroom. They are a powerful tool and their implications on syllabus content are extensive. They should not be viewed, however, as an isolated component of the mathematics curriculum. They, like other resources, should be seen and used as vehicles for mathematical enquiry to support the mathematical development of our pupils.

In this Introduction we outline:

A.    **The emphases of the project** (below)

B.    **The research process** (pages 6–7)

C.    **The nature, structure and possible use of the report** (pages 8–9).

## SECTION A    THE EMPHASES OF THE PROJECT

"A mathematical classroom can leave memories of excited and exciting discussions, of a varied pattern in its patchwork of learning, of fascination in the revelations of number and shape and of deep personal satisfaction in the defeat of a problem."

(*Teaching Mathematics in Secondary Schools*, HMSO 1958)

". . . scholars will thus be trained at an early age to use their intelligence, and not to place undue reliance upon the mechanical application of general methods."

(*Suggestions for the Consideration of Teachers*, Board of Education 1905)

". . . teachers should restrict themselves to giving children facility only in such mathematical skills as they can use and see the point of using."

(*Handbook of Suggestions for Teachers*, HMSO 1937)

". . . teaching should, in the main, be based upon the child's own experience and previous knowledge and . . . upon definite experiments made by him with concrete objects."

(*The Teaching of Arithmetic in London Elementary Schools*, LCC 1911)

"The exercises in reasoning afforded by arithmetic can have their full value or force only when the *child himself* investigates and draws inferences – when he fully realises the conditions of the problem, and is able to search for ways and means of solving it."

(*The Teaching of Arithmetic*, A. Monteith, Harrap 1928)

Statements of this kind have been made for a very long time by those concerned for the mathematical development of children, yet these assertions are still with us and even considered 'innovative' and 'new'. However, it is not difficult to find classrooms where children still:

- lack confidence in the subject;

- spend a majority of their time reproducing their teachers' examples with different numbers;

- answer only other people's questions;

- ask, 'What am I supposed to be doing then?';

- fail to connect their mathematics with other subjects or with their life outside school, even when they are successful in their mathematics lessons;

- dislike mathematics, seeing it as irrelevant and boring;

- spend most of their time mystified.

Even when reports have spelt out what 'needs to be done', and texts, schemes and syllabuses have clear aims and introduce new material or organisation, the depressing picture often persists. *See Chapters 2 and 3 – 'Children Learning Mathematics' and 'Aims and Actions'.*

Although students on initial training courses may have firm beliefs derived from their own experience about how to encourage mathematics learning, they often undergo a form of 'retraining' when they get into schools where an attitude of 'This is real life, you can forget what they told you in college' may exist. A probationary teacher wrote:

"I have started my probationary year with the conviction that I shall strive to make mathematics for my classes like it has been for me at College.

I want the children to experience pushing forward, trying out and modifying their own mathematical thinking rather than merely digesting and subsequently practising other people's smoothed out and polished ideas. I want them to be able to ask their own questions; to cover 'content' through their own explorations; to focus on connections and relationships rather than on isolated ideas and skills; to have opportunities to follow up their own interests; to think of actively interpreting other people's mathematics rather than passively absorbing it; to acquire confidence in their own abilities and feel the power of extending and controlling what they do.

But my intentions are frustrated by a range of things. Among others, they include:

– a weekly computation paper which emphasises what the children cannot do;

– time consuming form filling which leaves me little time to concentrate on planning how to involve children in inquiring for themselves;

– detailed record sheets of some eighty items all concerned with number, which include things like 'Division of hundreds, tens and units by units without exchange'.

And the irony is that all this has been thought out with the children's interests firmly at heart!"

Thus, if improvements in the learning of mathematics are to be widespread, it is inevitable that sustained change must begin with teachers themselves. Their beliefs about the nature of mathematics, how children learn and about their own role, are crucial factors in determining what actually happens in the classroom and therefore in determining the quality of children's mathematical development. Hence, any in-service provision that does not recognise these factors and merely 'tells' teachers what to do without enabling them to re-examine their beliefs based on their own experiences is unlikely to provide a platform for sustained teacher development.

A college lecturer indicated that:

"When courses fail to lead teachers to ways of mustering their own resources to meet new challenges, then they have little alternative but to accept the leadership and authority of others.

A teacher from a mathematics working group epitomises for me this renunciation of personal autonomy:

Teacher: 'Is what I'm doing right, and what should I be doing next?'"

If awareness, independence and confidence are to be increased, in-service provision must concentrate on drawing out the resources that exist within teachers.

A teacher who had been on a one-day-a-week course for a year wrote:

"The course has helped me to solve a lot of my problems about teaching maths by making the subject interesting to both pupils and teachers, and it has changed my whole outlook to teaching CDT as well.

I find I can lead pupils to discovering things by asking questions like, 'What happens if you do that?' or 'Why does it always work?' and so on.

I myself am seeing mathematics in more situations and using them in my teaching."

Teachers who are encouraged over a sustained period to challenge their own beliefs, experiment in their classrooms and share their experiences with colleagues will become more discriminating consumers of in-service provision, published materials and other resources. *See Chapter 4 – 'Teacher Development'.*

Many previous curriculum development projects in mathematics have provided these ingredients for the groups of teachers involved. The need to disseminate widely has led them to publish books and schemes with the genuine intention of sharing their work and helping the largest possible number of teachers. The teachers who receive the material, however, can only use it in accordance with their own convictions as to what should go on in a mathematics classroom. They are detached from the original source of inspiration and commitment. This can result in the material being misunderstood, essential features ignored and the quality of mathematics learning being little changed. Thus, if widespread dissemination is to be effective, detachment of this kind must be avoided. *See Chapters 5 and 6 – 'Widespread, Sustained Curriculum Development' and 'Schemes'.*

Other subject teachers' perceptions of mathematics often influence the way the subject is used and referred to in their disciplines. If improvements in mathematics are to be widespread then there are actions to be taken with respect to 'whole school policies' and cross-curricular cooperation. *See Chapter 7 – 'Working Across the Curriculum'.*

There exist many pressures which are viewed by teachers as 'external' and seen to be factors which ultimately determine what goes on in schools. Many teachers have listed such pressures as obstacles to change (see page 2). Concerns about parents, employers and assessment are often high on these lists. *See Chapter 8 – 'Evaluating and Assessing Mathematics' and Chapter 9 – 'Parents'.*

There is recognised national support in this country for a radical reappraisal of our mathematics curriculum. The Cockcroft enquiry and subsequent examination initiatives, for example GCSE and the Certificate of Pre-Vocational Education (CPVE), support teacher-initiated development. It is therefore significant that although there is this recognition 'from above', issues concerning syllabuses, examinations and others are still perceived by teachers at all levels, including headteachers and senior management, as external pressures that inhibit change in their classrooms. Clearly, important as these broad opportunities are, it is not enough that they simply exist. Teachers who have become more confident about what they are doing in their classrooms to enable their pupils to learn more effectively have taken these problems on as part of their overall professional responsibility. For these teachers the external pressures have lost their inhibiting effect. There exist, for example, many teachers whose perceptions of external restrictions have changed and who:

- do not view the syllabus as 'something to be got through', but as a broad indication of areas to explore. *(See Chapter 2 – 'Children Learning Mathematics')*
- have involved their headteachers in their classrooms and hence secured their financial, organisational and moral support. *(See Chapters 3 and 4 – 'Aims and Actions' and 'Teacher Development')*

- have created their own Mode 3 examinations that reflect and support the work in their classrooms. (The overriding principle of teacher involvement in assessment, which is inherent in GCSE, is encouraging this kind of development. *(See Chapter 8 – 'Evaluating and Assessing Mathematics')*

- have directly involved parents in mathematics and gained their support. *(See Chapter 9 – 'Parents')*

- have supported the professional development of non-specialist and probationary teachers in their departments through collaborative work, feedback and discussion rather than through prescriptive guidelines. *(See Chapter 6 – 'Schemes')*

- have manipulated the timetable to allow departments to have regular (for example fortnightly) days free of teaching commitment in order that they can meet and work together in school time. *(See Chapter 4 – 'Teacher Development')*

The kind of professional development that this report advocates enables teachers to become more confident and effective in their classrooms, and therefore more able and willing to take advantage of the broad opportunities available. Any short cuts are a false economy. The process is long-term and continuous. Time must be made available to teachers for this process. This development time needs to be seen as part of the 'everyday job of teaching'.

## SECTION B    THE RESEARCH PROCESS

In the original aims of the Project (*see Project Review*) the stress was placed on improving action in the classroom. Phrases such as the following occurred:

> to develop good practice . . . ;
> to change attitudes . . . ;
> to help to interpret . . . ;
> to gain insight . . . ;
> to enable pupils to . . . ;
> to develop ways of working that . . . .

Classroom life is complex. For the Project's aim of improved mathematics teaching and learning to be realised, any actions taken had to be embedded within this complex situation. Thus the authority for carrying out research and development lay with teachers in the classroom. It was necessary to sustain the contact with all the day-to-day problems of school life, such as difficult pupils and conditions, report writing, examinations and marking. To step back in the interests of 'objectivity' and to ignore these awkward realities of classroom life would have invalidated both the procedure and the outcomes of the Project's work.

The 12 teacher–researchers from the six Local Education Authorities (Dorset, East Sussex, Hampshire, Isle of Wight, Surrey and West Sussex) were freed from their teaching responsibilities for one day a week. On this day they worked in a number of ways including:

- working together, discussing, sharing and reflecting on classroom experiences both successful and unsuccessful;

- working in groups focusing on specific issues, including the examination of a number of previous relevant curriculum development and research projects, both in mathematics and in other curriculum areas;

- developing strategies for in-service work in their schools and with other teachers;
- exploring mathematical situations and evaluating possible outcomes;
- evaluating the effectiveness of commercial resources in the classroom;
- exploring the creative use of microcomputers in the mathematics classroom;
- working with other teachers on in-service courses;
- working with other teachers in their classrooms.

On their four days in school the teacher–researchers explored possibilities and ideas within their own classrooms, involved their colleagues through discussion and collaborative teaching and kept personal records. An important ongoing strategy the Project continues to employ involves individuals writing and talking about their own situations and experiences in a personal and uninhibited way. These 'case studies', and extracts from them, prove invaluable to other teachers. By their nature they are not prescriptive. Within each experience there are ingredients which other teachers may identify as being transferable to their own classroom. As a result they are encouraged to try out ideas with their own pupils. When groups of teachers come together in this way to pool their strategies and experiences their individual options are increased and useful common features emerge that help to isolate elements such as teacher personality that are not necessarily transferable. Through such discussion and personal experimentation the processes of questioning, experimenting, reflecting and evaluating become embedded in a teacher's practice. These processes become a continuous research cycle where evaluation leads to further questioning, which leads to further experimentation, reflection, evaluation and so on. This cycle is far from being a 'clinical' or 'academic' one. For teachers to reflect so intensely on their own classroom practice, beliefs and assumptions, both individually and in working groups, involves a good deal of emotional investment. It became clear that the focus of the Project was this way of working; a process which enables teachers to become more aware, discerning, confident and resourceful. The process pervades all the Project's in-service work. Further, the strategies it embodies are similar to those employed by teachers in classrooms to facilitate children's mathematical development because pupils also need to be involved in questioning, experimenting, reflecting and evaluating their mathematics in order to become more aware, discerning, confident and resourceful. *See Chapters 2 and 4 – 'Children Learning Mathematics' and 'Teacher Development'.*

Large numbers of teachers throughout the Project authorities are engaged in working with other teachers and with their pupils in this way. (For example, those on past and present courses associated with the Mathematics Centre at WSIHE and those involved in support and working groups in the region.) As a result the Project has a large, varied and continuously growing accumulation of knowledge and experience covering all aspects of the mathematics curriculum. Hence, *all* these teachers are part of the Project. Their work is an integral part of the research. They too are 'teacher–researchers'. This large group of teachers form a network which grows as teachers make new contacts and form new working groups throughout the region. The Project provides a focus enabling connections to be made between the various groups, which draw and feed from each other – a cellular growth model of expansion. This necessitates that all dissemination is through active personal involvement and contact, ensuring that curriculum development and research is firmly rooted in the personal experiences of teachers in their classrooms. *See Chapter 5 – 'Widespread, Sustained Curriculum Development'.*

**1.**   **The nature of the report.**

The nature of the Project's work necessitates that:

- this report is not 'the Project' itself. The ongoing work being done by teachers with other teachers and their pupils is 'the Project'. This is described above and in more detail in the following chapters;

- this report is not a 'write-up' by the Project Director. The report is a distillation of the experiences and knowledge of the large numbers of teachers and others who are involved;

- the report does not use quotations from external sources. Although it has an extensive bibliography of useful reading, all quotations used are from the large body of writing generated by those involved with the Project, including teachers, pupils, advisory staff, employers, college staff and parents from the six Local Education Authorities;

- this report alone cannot bring about widespread change in schools. Effective change can only come about by development of the kind we have described. *(See Chapter 3 – 'Aims and Actions'.)* Ways in which this document might be used as an in-service resource are discussed later;

- the strong recommendations and statements made throughout this report are based on the knowledge and reflect the wide experience of all those who are involved.

**2.**   **Some points concerning the structure of the report.**

Each chapter of the report considers a major focus and emphasis of the Project's work, and aims to some extent to be self-contained.

Points considered of particular significance are presented as bold lettered 'statements' and numbered 1 to 37.

The quotations in the report are not simply illustrative. They contain important points and in many ways may be considered the main part of the text.

Each chapter concludes with a summary, outlining the situation at present and recommendations for action. Many of the points in the recommendations section have already been implemented in individual schools in the region. *(See Project Review for more details.)*

## 3. Some ideas for using the report.

During the development and writing of this report, draft chapters have been circulated to a large number and a wide variety of people for comment, discussion and feedback. Many of these individuals and groups have been using them as an in-service resource. Some of the strategies they have used are below.

- The 'statements' in the report have been used as generalisations to be refuted. For example a Project member wrote about what happened when she used Statement 4.

**STATEMENT 4**
**Mathematics is effectively learned only by experimenting, questioning, reflecting, discovering, inventing and discussing. Thus, for children, mathematics should be a kind of learning which requires a minimum of factual knowledge and a great deal of experience in dealing with situations using particular kinds of thinking skills.**

"I offered the teachers the statement and asked them to pinpoint any areas of disagreement. They had to provide concrete, personal examples to back up their point of view. No second-hand stories or myths were allowed.

After some small group discussion there was a feeling that the word 'only' in the statement was wrong. Many teachers gave their own schooling as examples. They said *they* had been taught without any experimentation in their grammar schools and yet had learned mathematics effectively.

After some probing and discussion they decided there was more to 'experimentation' and 'discovering' than 'scissors and paste'. They identified that this had often taken place outside classtime, with friends, or on their own when experimentation and reflection were internalised.

By the end of the session many wanted the word 'only' underlined, and everyone had benefited from the discussion."

- Individual chapters have been used as a focus and a stimulus when teachers at all levels have come together to discuss and plan particular courses of action.

- Ideas from the chapters have been explored. For example, from Chapter 2 – 'Children Learning Mathematics', it has been found useful to invite teachers to make up their own list of 'What makes a rich mathematical activity' (page 20). Similarly, much discussion has developed when teachers have compiled their own lists of classroom actions that restrict or facilitate pupils' mathematical development (pages 17–19).

There is potential throughout the report for developing in-service activities of the kind above. For example in Chapter 6 – 'Schemes' (page 49) one teacher writes of his 'horror stories'; asking teachers to write or discuss theirs may prove fruitful. Chapter 8 – 'Evaluating and Assessing Mathematics' (page 69) refers to a teacher asking pupils for their opinions as to the 'best way of finding out how good they are at mathematics'. Collecting such responses from pupils may well provide a useful starting point for a departmental session on assessment.

All the starting points above provide a stimulus and focus, enabling those involved to discuss, challenge assumptions, reflect on experiences and plan future actions.

# 2

# CHILDREN LEARNING
# MATHEMATICS

Some pupils wrote about their perceptions of mathematics:

Mathematics is about learning to do. Sumes and to do fractions and angles

Mathematics is about thinking, its about working things out.

Mathematics is about ............ Finding theories and formula to link together certain problems, so as to find an answer to all areas releating to those problems. Finding links and patterns between puzzles and questions, leading up to a solution, so we can use that formla to work out all releated queries.
Mathematics is borderless, and does not just stop at numbers and number releated topics, such as algebra. But shapes, sizes and all sorts of things.

mathematics is about learning how to count, add, subtract, times and divide

mathsmatis strains your brain to the extream

for little children - money and clocks.

It is about learning to find the area of something

Algebra Mesuration, geometry Trigonametry, Graphs, Sets, Statistics and prabability and calculus.

I think maths is a problem waiting to be answered

**STATEMENT 1**
**Most difficulties in mathematics teaching hinge on the perception by pupils, teachers and parents of the nature and purpose of the mathematics in which they are engaged.**

Mathematics has enjoyed prestige as a subject for a very long time. Sometimes this has bordered on notoriety (try telling people at a party that you teach mathematics), but more often it has been viewed with some awe.

'It's hard and shows that you are clever.'

There is, however, a wide range of definitions as to what mathematics is. Some of these definitions are matters for philosophy, some come down from the perceived needs of industry, science and other disciplines. More of them have historical origins, often in social contexts such as 'public school scholarships' and 'elementary school arithmetic'. Indeed most people's perceptions of mathematics are shaped by the way they were taught the subject at school.

A lecturer in mathematics wrote of the public's perceptions of his subject:

"When pleasurable and effective, mathematics is not easily noticed. It can even be described as common sense. Only when unpleasant is it identified as mathematics.

Coexistent with this notion is that which depicts the 'professor of mathematics' as a comic figure, totally unpractical and divorced from reality, unable to cope with directions or small change or timetables or the like.

The contrast with literature and other aspects of science and the arts is striking:

Fun/popular/amateur-inventive science IS science.

Fun/popular/amateur-inventive mathematics IS NOT 'proper' mathematics."

Mathematics seems to be understood by most people to be a body of established knowledge and procedures – facts and rules. This describes the forms in which we observe mathematics in calculations, proofs and standard methods. However, most mathematicians would see this as a very narrow view of their subject. It denies the value of mathematics as an activity in which to engage. Decision making, experimenting, hypothesising, generalising, modelling, communicating, interpreting, proving, symbolising and pattern finding are all integral parts of that activity. Without engaging in processes such as these, no mathematician would have been able to create the procedures and systems mentioned above in the first place.

A mathematics teacher noted:

"I have spent many years in schools, and fairly consistently found that I gained much from teachers of art, of music, of crafts. I realised that much of their success, and value, was probably due to the fact that they were usually 'practising' their subjects – they painted, they played, they designed. I think I am persuaded that it is equally important for mathematics teachers to be doing some mathematics themselves, experiencing some of the pleasures and pains, frustrations and fears, which their classes should also be feeling."

**STATEMENT 2**
**Teacher enthusiasm for and personal engagement in the processes of mathematics will greatly enhance the mathematical experiences of their pupils.**

Because of the unquestioned inclusion of mathematics in the school curriculum, most teachers of the subject are not required to justify its place and purpose to pupils, parents or colleagues. It is often the case that teachers have never had the opportunity to examine and sharpen their beliefs about the nature of mathematics.

A teacher wrote of his changed perceptions of the subject:

"From my own point of view I have certainly changed my view as to 'what is mathematics'. I suppose that I had accepted a very restricted view of a number of mathematical topics – the syllabus – rather than considering the processes going on. By syllabus, I suppose I also restricted myself to an 'exam' syllabus – my teaching stemmed from there. I do feel that because I am changing, because I am realising the necessity of observing what is happening in the classroom in a real sense, rather than just whether Johnny is managing to get 4 when adding 2 and 2 – because my realisation of what mathematics is about is changing, the attitudes adopted by my pupils are changing too."

We have found the following implications when teachers' perceptions about the nature of mathematics have broadened:

**A.**  Teachers have gained insight into how children learn mathematics (below).

**B.**  This has had radical implications with respect to the teacher's role in the mathematics classroom (pages 16–20).

**C.**  Teachers and their pupils have derived more success and pleasure from the subject (pages 21–22).

## A.  How children learn mathematics.

Two pupils wrote:

I enjoy most problems in Maths because it gives a good challenge for me.

Some of the problems are a good challange witch I like but if it is too hard you are aloud to make it easyer. I would like maths to carry on like this next year because it makes you think

It is often the case that the mathematical diet for low attaining pupils consists of little more than basic arithmetic, presented in simple step by step learning sequences, and repeated frequently. This is usually because it is felt that they cannot cope with anything at a higher level or with more demanding work. Many teachers have found, however, that this diet does not enable their pupils to succeed. They find their pupils saying that they do not understand a topic after they have met it over and over again. They find them getting bored with meeting work they have been doing, with varying degrees of success, since primary school. Teachers talk of their pupils' inability to concentrate, and their inability to decide which operations to use in different contexts. However, when teachers have presented these pupils with a broader based mathematical challenge, they have found them actually achieving more. The pupils *can* cope with the frustrations and floundering inherent in such challenges provided it is in a supportive atmosphere or environment, where the process of struggle is viewed as successful in itself.

**STATEMENT 3**
**In many cases low attainment is a direct result of the restricted and unfulfilling nature of the work pupils are given. They** *need* **challenges to get their teeth into.**

This food analogy was taken further by a college lecturer associated with the Project:

## FOOD FOR THOUGHT

| JUNK FOOD | JUNK MATHEMATICS |
|---|---|
| There is a lot of it about. | See most school textbooks. |
| All the preparation is done for you by someone else. | This is done by the author or teacher – all the nasties are removed. |
| The instructions for use are simple and laid out in steps. | See most textbook questions. |
| It is superficially attractive but turns out to lack flavour. | It looks well structured and appears logical, but is dull and lacks substance. |
| It does you little good; it tends to pass through quickly. | Pupils are unable to retain or apply it in new contexts. |
| All the real nutrient is removed and substitutes have to be added. | It offers no real life situations but invents and contrives them. |

**DANGER: HEALTH WARNING**
**Junk mathematics can seriously damage your pupils.**

If children are to obtain genuine 'nourishment' from their mathematical diet, it has to be freed from the artificial way in which it is presented. A teacher wrote:

"Generally we interchange (wrongly) learning with remembering, yet if real learning occurred would we as teachers need to spend so much time on revision programmes? Mathematics has also come to mean right and wrong; there is thus little room for individualised thinking, no room for an opinion. Rules are taught to be remembered. The methods are as archaic as making children recall a 30 line poem – gone is the beauty, the meaning and the enjoyment. All that remains is the fear of forgetting a verse."

It is certainly the case that in most mathematics lessons pupils are taught the rules, technical notations and established conventions of mathematics without acquiring any feeling for why these systems exist. To teach the subject in this way is to obscure the main reasons why people have enjoyed making and using mathematics, and to deny pupils the experience of actually doing mathematics themselves.

The comparisons possible with other areas of the curriculum are enlightening:

*Is drama to be taught from the published text without ever seeing a play, trying to perform one, or trying to extemporise or write one?*

*Is music to be taught from the score, explaining rules, constructions, notational devices and musical vocabulary without hearing or playing the sound for which the syntax exists?*

*Now that we can produce symbolised choreography, do we spend all our time teaching the symbol system so that children will be able to dance when they leave school?*

*Are children in art lessons to be taught about different paints and media, and shown other people's paintings without putting brush on paper or hands on clay?*

A teacher wrote:

"Relying on a set of rules taught by the teacher is only as good as the child's memory allows for instant and accurate recall. We all know the problem of trying to remember a lot of unrelated facts; they become mixed and muddled for the majority."

Can we justify the teacher saying things like:

'Line up all the dots and start at the right.'

'Take out the decimal point, count the number of numbers behind the point, then stick it back in.'

'Two minuses make a plus.'

'It's a ten, so we put a nought down first.'

'Take it over and change the sign.'

'Just add a nought.'

Children must find their own strategies so that they can apply them appropriately, and understand established rules for what they are. 'I've forgotten how to do long multiplication' may well mean, 'I've forgotten *your* rule for multiplying two big numbers together'. The more we teach algorithms the more inflexible children are likely to become.

A teacher described this incident with his bottom set, second years:

"In this, the second lesson, the children were working on their own variations of a number chain. Mary had decided to *divide* each number by itself instead of multiplying.

I watched from a distance as she dutifully plugged her numbers into a calculator and kept getting the answer 1. She looked genuinely surprised and tried at some very big numbers to test her theory. After that she leapt from her chair and ran to me saying 'I've made an incredible discovery! If you divide a number by itself you *ALWAYS* get 1, no matter what number you use.'

We then had a discussion about why that should be and it became obvious she really understood. She was so thrilled with this discovery she insisted on explaining it to the rest of the class.

This incident left me both depressed and encouraged. I was depressed because I had assumed from all the division work we had done in the first year that Mary already knew that x divided by x is 1. I was encouraged because (a) now I am convinced she does know it and therefore won't forget it, and (b) that it was the open situation in the classroom that enabled her to experiment and therefore find it out in *her* way, not mine."

**STATEMENT 4**
**Mathematics is effectively learned only by experimenting, questioning, reflecting, discovering, inventing and discussing.**
**Thus, for children, mathematics should be a kind of learning which requires a minimum of factual knowledge and a great deal of experience in dealing with situations using particular kinds of thinking skills.**

## B.  The teacher's role in the mathematics classroom.

Perceptions about children's learning have enormous implications for actions taken by teachers in classrooms.

Consider the following contrasting lists:

| LIST A | LIST B |
|---|---|
| Pupils dislike mathematics and will avoid it if they can. | Children freely engage in activities that are essentially mathematical. |
| Pupils want to be told what to do and be directed towards appropriate tasks. | Pupils are able to identify and direct themselves towards appropriate tasks. |
| Pupils are mainly motivated by teacher approval, a desire to succeed at examinations, or to achieve 'tokens of merit'. | Pupils can become fascinated by mathematical contradictions and absurdities and are motivated by mathematical activity itself. |
| Most pupils have little creativity or imagination, except when it comes to thinking of excuses for not having done their homework. | Creativity and ingenuity are widely distributed and evident in the natural activities of children outside school. |
| There are identifiable skills which the teacher knows and which need to be explained to the children and practised so that they are well equipped for life. | The mastery of skills is of little use if they cannot be applied. The skills pupils need are the strategies of problem solving; interpreting mathematical forms and statements; representing situations mathematically. These must be developed in context, through experience. |
| Pupils need clear step-by-step explanations in order to avoid confusion. | A state of temporary confusion or puzzlement is at the heart of all learning. |
| Pupils are empty vessels waiting to be filled from the teacher's expert stock of knowledge. | Pupils bring their own knowledge and experience and need to be actively involved in their mathematical development. |

The caricature of teacher beliefs in List A would give rise to a correspondingly narrow set of teacher actions, whereas a teacher characterised by List B may well have a wider range of teaching strategies available. *More about the implications of teachers' beliefs can be found in Chapter 4 – 'Teacher Development'.*

The commonly held view that good teachers are ones who can pass on their expertise through clear explanations so as to avoid confusing their pupils has some interesting implications.

- *The view implies that:* the teacher is the holder of answers in a classroom, one who knows the answers to all of the pupils' questions. In a classroom where such an answer-orientated atmosphere exists, it is difficult to imagine much exploration into unknown territory taking place, as pupils will find it difficult to believe that there are areas where their teacher does not 'know the answer'. This leads to a marked lack of independence on behalf of pupils as is evidenced by their cries of 'Is this right?' or 'Where's the answer book?' This atmosphere also helps to perpetuate the view of mathematics where the only problems are those with a right or wrong answer, or a right or wrong method.

**STATEMENT 5**
**The more solutions and strategies pupils see and discuss, the more likely they are to develop a real appreciation of mathematics at their own level.**

- *The view implies that:* the teacher is seen by pupils as having total responsibility for leading and controlling the work that is going on in the classroom. We have found that because pupils rarely get the chance to use their own initiative they become even more dependent on their teacher for direction. Staffroom complaints about fifth years still having to be 'spoon fed' are therefore not really surprising. This 'teacher authority' can lead to pupils being stifled by their teachers' expectations.

This teacher highlights the problem:

"In developing work in the classroom one's own expectations and experiences often interfere with a child's progress and it is important to be aware of this and exercise self control.

My main aim is to direct their work as little as possible, letting them find their own system and choose their own path to follow. I am not advocating no guidance though, since a teacher's role in this respect is a vital one, but it can easily be overdone and destroy a sense of personal achievement.

This requires cutting the instructions to a bare minimum, so that you are, in effect, just providing them with the seed of an idea, and allowing them to culture it."

- *The view implies that:* in a climate of teacher expertise, well defined methods and careful explanations, teachers often feel obliged to provide clever tricks to short cut the processes of decision making, choice of procedure and securing conviction or proof, often thinking that this is necessary in order to 'get through the syllabus'. Teachers frequently pre-empt pupils' decisions because they do not want them to 'get into a mess'. Their enthusiasm to convey solutions to pupils often ends up by precluding the pupils' own ideas and can be not only inhibiting but also take away the pupils' enjoyment of getting there themselves.

In our efforts to make things easier for our pupils we often act in other inhibiting ways. Five common classroom actions that restrict pupils' mathematical development are outlined below:

1. *The subject is broken down into 'easily digestible topics'.* Teachers often lament that pupils do not see and use links between different areas of the subject. When it is considered that in the 'real world' mathematics does not come in the small

fragmented packages that so frequently exist on our syllabuses (eg 'Perimeter' and 'Area'), it is not surprising that pupils are unable to get a useful overview, or see relationships.

2. *There is an over-concern to simplify, by breaking general ideas into seemingly unrelated stages.* The point of the overall task in hand is often obscured when step-by-step instructions are provided, for example when a pupil neatly sets out a long multiplication sum in order to multiply by 100.

3. *Difficulties are smoothed out for pupils by, for example, ensuring that awkward cases do not occur or that the numbers cancel or that the answer is not a fraction.* This presents a false view of the subject and can lead to the situation where unusual extensions of these easier cases are not recognised. It also restricts opportunities for pupils' own interesting mathematical questions of the kind below:

> 'What is infinity plus one?'

> 'Is 0 a number?'

> 'What's the square root of a minus number then?'

> 'What does this – mean on my calculator?'

4. *It is often assumed that techniques must be learned and practised before problems are mentioned.* This can lead to a lack of motivation, as well as to a lack of understanding and meaning. When pupils complain that they 'don't see the point of doing all these', they are often given a remote justification – 'You'll need it when you buy a carpet'.

5. *An idea that arises naturally or that has a ready-made context is often unconsciously mystified by over-explanation/exposition.* For example, spending a great deal of time and effort arriving at a rule for rounding off money to the nearest pound. Once again this can lead not only to confusion, but also to a loss of purpose and motivation.

Teachers need to be seen by pupils to be genuinely interested in their mathematical ideas. We have found that this encourages children to ask and answer their own questions. There is a wealth of strategies for enabling pupils to do more of the thinking in mathematics lessons. The range of possible choices develops when teachers work together, sharing their failures and successes, and pooling their ideas for improving their pupils' mathematical experiences. *(See Chapter 4 – 'Teacher Development'.)*

A head of department wrote down some of her strategies:

"I feel that I *must:*

STOP myself from telling children the answers too often;

try to limit the number of times I interrupt or interfere when children are quite happy working;

allow time for 'talking' mathematics and not discourage lively class activities/ discussions because they might be 'noisy';

allow children to 'take off' without worrying how I'm going to mark their work or check it;

allow children to do messy activities such as painting, glueing and cutting;

STOP worrying about the end result too early;

STOP worrying when things don't go according to plan;

KEEP trying to modify approaches without feeling too discouraged.

Incorporating ANY idea in the classroom is a complex problem. There has to be trial and error and modification in the light of experience – there must be sharing with other teachers of successes and failures. I MUST NOT EXPECT TOO MUCH TOO SOON."

Since the Cockcroft Report the word 'investigation' has taken on enormous significance in the minds of mathematics teachers around the country. However, in many cases the spirit behind investigative activity in the mathematics classroom has been lost. This is evidenced by teachers asking questions like "How much time am I supposed to spend doing investigations?". For them the word 'investigation' refers not to an attitude pervading all their teaching, but to a new and additional 'topic' to be covered on their syllabus, with identifiable labels like 'Frogs' or 'Happy Numbers'. If pupils are to benefit in the ways we have indicated in this chapter then, although activities such as 'Frogs' or 'Happy Numbers' can be excellent starting points for exploration, it is essential that a spirit of enquiry is seen to permeate the whole of mathematics teaching and learning.

A group of teachers on an in-service course attempted to draw up a list describing necessary ingredients for a rich mathematical activity:

### WHAT MAKES A RICH MATHEMATICAL ACTIVITY?

- **It must be accessible to everyone at the start.**

- **It needs to allow further challenges and be extendible.**

- **It should invite children to make decisions.**

- **It should involve children in speculating, hypothesis making and testing, proving or explaining, reflecting, interpreting.**

- **It should not restrict pupils from searching in other directions.**

- **It should promote discussion and communication.**

- **It should encourage originality/ invention.**

- **It should encourage 'what if' and 'what if not' questions.**

- **It should have an element of surprise.**

- **It should be enjoyable.**

They then went on to pool ideas on strategies for generating mathematical enquiry:

START WITH EXPLORATORY TYPE QUESTIONS LIKE:

HOW MANY DIFFERENT
. . . . . . . .ways to work out $21 \times 13$? . . . . . . . .ways to satisfy $c = a + 2b$? . . . . . . . .ways to draw an equilateral triangle?

WHAT HAPPENS WHEN . . . . . . . .?      CAN YOU FIND A BETTER WAY . . . . . . . .?

IS IT TRUE THAT
. . . . . . . .12% of £40 is the same as 40% of £12?

GET PUPILS TO SET THEIR OWN QUESTIONS
. . . . . . . .pass them around.

ASK THEM TO FIND OUT HOW TO DO SOMETHING
. . . . . . . .find the area of a triangle. . . . . . . . .construct a 30 degree angle.

START WITH A PROBLEM OR DILEMMA
. . . . . . . .explore. . . . . . . . .sort out the contradictions or confusions.

START WITH AN ANSWER
. . . . . . .explore. . . . . . . .how did they get it? . . . . . . . .what was the question/problem?
. . . . . . .what's gone wrong?

USE AN OUTSIDE STIMULUS
. . . . . . . .radio/TV/newspaper puzzles. . . . . . . . .advertisements. . . . . . . .familiar everyday anomalies.

GET PUPILS TO MAKE OR INVENT SOMETHING
. . . . . . . .to measure turn. . . . . . . . .to measure time. . . . . . . . .to carry a certain weight.

USE GAMES
. . . . . . . .can they make them harder? . . . . . . .can they understand each others' rules?

**C. Teachers and their pupils have derived more success and pleasure from the subject.**

Some pupils wrote:

Maths is interesting when ........ the teacher does not go "waffle, waffle, waffle .. page 64 Exercise A, B, C, D " It's different in this class because we don't just do routine work, we practise something that is very important — thinking.

..the bottom set does all sorts of intresting things and they find out loks of information and I feel so sorry for the top set because they have to copy pages and pages of work out of the maths book

I think it gives us a very good chance to do better. I like it because we are our own boss and we are much more independant. It is much better than staring at the teacher for a lesson or two. That can get terribly boring

When I done pages and pages of work I used to hate and dred going to the less ons. Now I like maths because we solve things

the reason I enjoyed it is because the begining of the work may have been set but then you had the freedom to work on the subject as you wanted to. The thing I learnt most is how to use and the meaning of mathmatical terms for example the decimal point and fractions

I think I have learnet that the more you find out theres always some thing to go on to

down our old school we allways did sums and you dont really find alot out in sums.

We have found that pupils and teachers have become more proficient and confident in their mathematics. When pupils have engaged in the subject in the ways we indicate in this chapter, they have become more able and willing to understand and tackle established procedures and rules and sort out mathematical confusions.

A pupil wrote:

> I used to be terrible at maths
> These lessons have given me much more confidence and now I understand things better. If somebody gave me a maths problem I would investigate the problem and I would be able to work it out.

Teachers who have broadened their range of teaching strategies have found that they are able to overcome the major problem of limiting children's attainment. Pupils at *all* levels are surpassing traditional expectations. Examination success and the take up of further courses in mathematics have both greatly increased.

**STATEMENT 6**
**Rich mathematical activities should enable**
***all* pupils to become engaged in motivating**
**and challenging work.**

In the raising of children's attainment and enjoyment we consider the following five factors significant:

1. *Dealing with failure and fear.*
A teacher wrote:

"Mathematics is a subject closely related to failure, and it is also socially acceptable to be bad at mathematics. I think that as long as educated people are not embarrassed but rather proud of their poor levels of competence then this will not alter."

It certainly seems absurd that highly educated and successful professionals happily admit that they are 'useless at maths'. The subject is extensively disliked and feared by children regardless of age, ability, and background. A teacher commented:

"One of my main aims is getting rid of this feeling of fear – fear of asking questions, fear of 'getting it wrong'."

When pupils are allowed the opportunities to engage in mathematics in the wider ways we have indicated, their enjoyment of the subject has increased. When pupils do their own mathematics it becomes significant for them. Success in such activities is usually very rewarding and includes a strong element of pleasure of the 'I've sorted it out myself' kind. This applies equally to those pupils who already enjoy mathematical activities as well as to those who have been numbed by past experience.

2. *Relevance*
It is often felt that children will succeed if what they do in the classroom relates to 'everyday life'. Whilst it is true that pupils do achieve more if they see their work as meaningful, the question of relevance is not an easy one, as this teacher points out:

"We are preoccupied with relevance, but what does this mean? Relevant to whom, and at what stage? Utilitarian skills are often thought to be important and presumed to be relevant, but do the students perceive them as such?

Hire-purchase calculations are thought to be relevant, but surely this is only so if you are considering purchasing something on H.P., and even then the salesman will probably do the calculations for you!

I believe that relevance occurs if the student is interested in what he or she is doing. In turn interest is generated by challenge and variety."

> **STATEMENT 7**
> **For mathematical activity to be meaningful, it needs to be personally fulfilling. This could either be because of its perceived relevance or because of its intrinsic fascination to the pupil/mathematician.**

### 3. *Skills and strategies*

If learning is 'effective' pupils should be able to use their mathematical ideas, skills and strategies in a variety of different contexts within the subject, in other curriculum areas and outside school. If children are to be able to cope with the diversity and ambiguity of real life problems, skills must not be taught in isolation, thus avoiding comments like, 'Is this an add, Miss?', and 'Do I times it first, Sir?'

### 4. *Initiative*

A teacher wrote:

"The pupils have started to take more responsibility themselves for what we do in the classroom. The work, although initiated by me, is taken through by them to a much greater extent than it used to be and that includes how and where they work. If they need more table space, they simply get more table space. As long as it is done in a sensible manner they know it will be accepted."

When pupils are allowed to take decisions for themselves, their organisational skills and initiative are developed and improved.

### 5. *Changing*

The changes in mathematics learning and teaching outlined in this chapter are not easy for teachers or pupils, as this teacher emphasises:

"It takes a group some considerable time to develop an enquiring approach. They do not generally expect to think for themselves – to be in a position to make decisions that will govern the directions of their study."

Changes need to be developed in an atmosphere of mutual trust and confidence. Issues relating to teacher change are considered in Chapter 4 – 'Teacher Development'. It is important that, if unnecessary antagonism is to be avoided, pupils are actively involved in implementing changes, and therefore understand what is happening.

Even those who have reached a traditionally high academic level can lack confidence in problem solving situations and show a marked lack of flexibility when it comes to using their mathematics creatively. Hence they too may be considered 'low attainers' in mathematics.

> **STATEMENT 8**
> **A change in a teacher's thinking about mathematics and learning in the ways we have indicated in this chapter has the potential to improve the attitudes and attainment of *all* the pupils he or she teaches, not just those of limited ability or those labelled 'low attainers'.**

## The situation

1. General perceptions of school mathematics are exceedingly narrow, and this is a major factor in inhibiting attempts to improve practice.

2. Attitudes and practice in mathematics are often markedly different from those in other subjects.

3. When teachers' perceptions about the nature of mathematics have broadened they have gained a greater insight into how children learn mathematics. This has had radical implications with respect to the teacher's role in the mathematics classroom.

4. In many cases low attainment is a direct result of the restricted and unfulfilling nature of the work pupils are given. They need challenges.

5. In most mathematics lessons pupils are taught the rules, technical notations and established conventions of mathematics without acquiring any feeling for why these systems exist. To teach the subject in this way is to obscure the main reasons why people have enjoyed making and using mathematics, and to deny pupils the experience of actually doing mathematics themselves.

6. The view of a teacher's role being merely to pass on expertise through clear explanations so as to avoid confusion leads directly to:
   (a) an answer oriented atmosphere in the classroom.
   (b) an overriding dependence on the teacher.
   (c) the inhibition of pupils' own ideas.
   (d) a fear of 'getting it wrong'.

7. Teachers' behaviour in classrooms can restrict pupils' mathematical development. Common sources of these 'inhibitors' are outlined in this chapter.

8. Through pressure since the Cockcroft Report, 'doing investigations' has become in many teachers' eyes another syllabus requirement – a bandwagon – thus losing the spirit behind an investigative approach.

9. An investigative approach to the subject, by its nature, necessitates a variety of teaching situations.

10. When pupils are allowed the opportunities to engage in mathematics in the wider ways we have indicated in this chapter, their enjoyment, confidence and attainment increase.

11. The changes in mathematics teaching and learning that we have outlined in this chapter have the potential to improve the attitudes and attainment of *all* pupils, not just those of limited ability or labelled 'low attainers'.

## Recommendations

1. Perceptions about the nature of mathematics need to be broadened. This is a fundamental prerequisite to the change outlined in this chapter. Teachers need time and support for this. See also Chapter 4 – 'Teacher Development' and Chapter 5 – 'Widespread, Sustained Curriculum Development'.

2. For pupils to achieve more, their mathematical diet must encompass challenge and active involvement in directing their own enquiries.

3. Mathematics can be effectively learned only by involving pupils in experimenting, questioning, reflecting, discovering, inventing and discussing. Mathematics should be a kind of learning which requires a minimum of factual knowledge and a great deal of experience in dealing with situations using particular kinds of thinking skills.

4. Collaborative work between teachers is a major factor in the development of strategies for generating and sustaining rich mathematical activity in the classroom. Provision for this is needed.

5. The changes in mathematics learning and teaching outlined in this chapter may not be easy for teachers or pupils, and must be developed in an atmosphere of mutual trust and confidence.

6. It is essential that if the spirit behind enquiry based learning is to be achieved in our mathematics classrooms, then teachers must understand and be in sympathy with the philosophy behind such teaching approaches. See also Chapter 4 – 'Teacher Development'.

# 3

# AIMS AND ACTIONS

A letter from a teacher began as follows:

"I am both furious and upset! I had done work on basic statistics with my second years. Although there is a tight syllabus to keep to I thought it a worthwhile exercise to get the children to do their own surveys in their homework time over a couple of weeks.

The children got a lot of pleasure from this and spent far longer than they would have on 'ordinary' homework – some even going to the lengths of typing out a questionnaire and duplicating it. I got the children to display their work and again many children were quite happy to spend breaks and lunchtimes doing this.

As the walls in my room were already full the children put up their work in the hall outside and this aroused considerable interest from other children – BUT . . . believe it or not my Head of Department got a note from the headmaster this morning complaining! He had criticised 3 spelling mistakes – He felt it did not reflect well on the school to have these. He also criticised the fact that work had been put on the wall and not on notice boards (there are none in the entrance hall)."

**STATEMENT 9**
**Aims for schools, departments and lessons often relate to choice, autonomy, self-motivation and confidence, as well as putting stress on the development of thinking individuals. Actions taken are often incompatible with these aims and sometimes are directly opposed to them.**

"Spelling boy, spelling!"

Enlightened aims in education are not peculiar to modern times. Recent Government reports have encouraged the profession generally to consider its aims at all levels. For some time now we have expected Local Education Authorities, heads of schools, heads of departments and individual teachers to prepare detailed aims. There seems to be an expectation that these aims will directly influence what happens in the classroom, act as instruments of curriculum change and form guidelines for teachers in, for example, the production of detailed syllabuses.

We have found a frequent mismatch between what is intended by those working in education at all levels, and what actions are taken in schools and classrooms. In some cases when we suggested that teachers might consult their school aims they were unable to obtain them. This unfortunate response came from a teacher:

> "I have been teaching at my present school
> for 20 years and I have never seen the
> school aims and as far as I know the school
> has no aims published."

Even when a document sets out recommended actions to implement its aims there is often incompatibility.

**STATEMENT 10**
**Aims can only act as forces for change and development when those who are to use and understand them are actively involved in either their evolution or in working at their implications as they affect their own situation.**

In many instances the production of a list of aims is a response to a pressure from above, rather than from a perceived internal need. When students are made to write them for their tutors, departments for their headteachers, headteachers for their governors and local authorities, and local authorities for external agencies, the involvement is often on a superficial level. As a result such aims are often treated unsympathetically and cynically by teachers as products of 'ivory tower thinking' unrelated to the practicalities of classroom life. Without a more meaningful involvement, aims can become misunderstood, misrepresented or even ignored.

Actions can also be at variance with aims when they mask larger 'hidden aims' reflecting ingrained social attitudes towards mathematics teaching. For example, the Cockcroft Committee's recommendation that pupils should be actively involved in discussing their mathematics cannot co-exist with the view that classrooms should always be quiet with pupils working on their own.

*The following aims from 'Mathematics from 5 to 16' and some common classroom actions illustrate this mismatch:*

## AIM

*"Mathematics as an essential element of communication.*

The mere manipulation of numerical or algebraic symbols is of secondary importance."

## ACTION

2. (a) $1.45 \times 2$ (b) $6.83 \times 8$ (c) $19.67 \times 7$ (d) $33.819 \times 9$ (e) $50.267 \times 5$

3. (a) $1.6 \times 30$ (b) $2.8 \times 60$ (c) $29.21 \times 90$ (d) $46.34 \times 70$ (e) $71.142 \times 40$

4. (a) $6.9 \times 72$ (b) $8.3 \times 84$ (c) $9.21 \times 43$ (d) $8.62 \times 27$ (e) $9.53 \times 18$

5. (a) $20.23 \times 57$ (b) $31.65 \times 62$ (c) $8.376 \times 94$ (d) $2.108 \times 39$ (e) $1.663 \times 81$

6. (a) $15.82 \times 10$ (b) $15.82 \times 100$ (c) $15.82 \times 1000$ (d) $1.582 \times 100$ (e) $1.582 \times 1000$

7. (a) $14.6 \times 0.2$ (b) $20.9 \times 0.7$ (c) $15.4 \times 1.2$ (d) $37.9 \times 2.3$ (e) $50.8 \times 3.5$

| AIM | ACTION |
|---|---|

*"Mathematics as a powerful tool.*

Skills such as measuring length, telling the time, constructing a graph, drawing geometric shapes, dividing one number by another and solving an equation are not important ends in themselves and only become so as they are embedded in purposeful activities."

'We must learn about different units so I want you all to measure your exercise books in centimetres, and then when you've done that we can measure the room using metres.'

*"Imagination, initiative and flexibility of mind in mathematics.*

When presented with a mathematical task pupils should be encouraged to find their own method of carrying it out even though there may be a standard, more streamlined method which they might ultimately learn."

'Now, even if you can do it without using the method, I still want you to use it because you'll need to know it for the harder ones later on.'

*"The aim should be to show mathematics as a process, as a creative activity in which pupils can be fully involved, and not as an imposed body of knowledge immune to any change or development."*

'Yes, I expect it would work that way, but now let's find out the right way to do it.'

*"Working independently.*

Success in teaching can be gauged, to some extent, by the way in which pupils have learnt to work effectively in an independent way."

'Now when you've finished that make sure you see me to get it marked. Then I'll give you the next bit.'

*"Working cooperatively.*

It means working together on a common task where all the pupils in the group make a contribution . . . This aim emphasises the interactive nature of mathematics; it should be less of a solitary experience than it is at present."

'I want you working quietly and on your own. After all if you copy someone else's work you are only cheating yourself in the end.'

*"In-depth study of mathematics.*

Much of the mathematical experience of most pupils is extremely fragmented, as they proceed from one small item to another in quick succession . . . An in-depth study is of potential value for all pupils, not only mathematically but also in terms of the development of personal qualities such as commitment and persistence."

'My pupils can only concentrate for ten minutes at a time so I give them work in small easily digestible topics with easy-to-follow step-by-step instructions.'

*"Pupils' confidence in their mathematical abilities.*

Mathematics must be an experience from which pupils derive pleasure and enjoyment."

'I know you don't like it, but its on the syllabus, so you'll need it for the exam.'

Mismatch occurs when aims hold no conviction for teachers. Their actions are in fact reflecting their own beliefs about mathematics teaching. These assumptions are reinforced over generations by popular myths relating to good practice in the subject. These powerful 'hidden aims' make it possible for teachers to reject ideas because they don't fit in with how they were taught or because the ideas are at odds with an imagined public view of mathematics and mathematics teaching. *These conflicts are examined further in Chapter 2 – 'Children Learning Mathematics' and Chapter 4 – 'Teacher Development'.*

As a further example of the complex relationship between aims and actions consider the following scenario:

An educational body concerned with improving pupils' awareness, thinking, communication and decision making skills sets out a group of laudable aims reflecting the above needs. They want them to be accessible to all teachers, and for all teachers to act on them, hence improving the mathematical lot of pupils.

There is concern, however, that teachers will not appreciate or have time to interpret the aims themselves in terms of classroom actions so a set of guidelines is produced.

Still little action is taken in schools – teachers are busy marking, preparing, writing reports and have not got the time or inclination to read through the guidelines. In an effort to make it easier for teachers to interpret these guidelines a checklist of desired actions is produced on which teachers can simply tick off items corresponding to good practice. This is appealing, offering comfort and security.

When the original aims are presented to teachers, on an occasional in-service day for instance, these are still not recognised. They may also be seen as irrelevant to their 'school life' and be received at best with indifference, at worst with antagonism and cynicism.

If actions are not to become detached from the original aims what needs to be done? Aims such as 'helping pupils to develop lively enquiring minds' have been restated in various curriculum documents over generations. Stating them again is not going to help teachers act on them. If we want teachers to use and act on such aims, diluting them into checklists and simple examples does not help either. Indeed this can lead to the situation where the task of filling in the checklist takes over and becomes an aim in itself.

When actions are seen not to match up with aims it is often assumed that teachers are not capable or willing to put them into practice. External efforts to remedy this can lead even further away from the original aim. For example, the aim of developing pupils' thinking skills has been corrupted in many cases into the teaching of separate 'study skills' lessons. The essence of the original aim, which was to encourage such skills throughout the curriculum, has in many instances been lost, as pupils become unable to transfer and apply these skills. A similar problem exists with the 'teaching' of 'life skills'. *(See Chapter 7 – 'Working across the Curriculum'.)*

We have found that when teachers are involved in working at the implications of aims and their associated actions these problems are minimised. One of the many in-service activities developed by the Project invited teachers to:
  (a) take an aim they wish to fulfil;
  (b) outline the classroom actions necessary to facilitate the aim;
  (c) consider the consequences or 'prices' of these actions.

When the consequences in (c) actually contradicted their original aim teachers considered further actions to remedy the situations and articulated arguments for the resources and priorities needed. Involvement in group activities of this kind has enabled teachers to use productively reports and curriculum documents previously available but inaccessible to them.

The letter at the beginning of this chapter demonstrates that there is still a problem for teachers attempting to put aims into practice. There will be a vital need for senior managements' organisational and moral support especially when teachers may be struggling for new strategies. However, this is not enough. Senior management also need to be involved as active participants in the process of examining the match between aims and actions.

*The issues of 'whole school policies' and support for teachers are considered in greater depth in Chapter 7 – 'Working across the Curriculum', Chapter 4 – 'Teacher Development' and Chapter 5 – 'Widespread, Sustained Curriculum Development'.*

## SUMMARY

### The situation

1. Aims for schools, departments and lessons often relate to choice, autonomy, self-motivation and confidence, as well as putting stress on the development of thinking individuals. Actions taken are often incompatible with these aims and sometimes are directly opposed to them.

2. There are enormous difficulties with regard to aims being translated into consistent actions.

3. In many instances the production of a list of aims is a response to a pressure from above, rather than from a perceived internal need.

4. Teachers do not relate to lists of aims in discussion and curriculum documents unless they have been personally involved in either evolving or actively working at the aims and their implications.

5. In an effort to simplify aims in order to help teachers interpret and realise them, teacher development is often inhibited. See also Chapter 4 – 'Teacher Development'.

### Recommendations

1. Those at *all* levels in education must be involved in the process of challenging the implications of aims and their associated actions. Time is needed for teachers to work together on such activities. This is not a one-day activity.

2. Senior management must believe in the importance of this teacher involvement and will need to be involved themselves as active participants rather than only as observers or organisers.

3. Support within school is essential. See also Chapter 4 – 'Teacher Development'.

# 4

# TEACHER DEVELOPMENT

A teacher on an in-service course wrote:

*"MY CHANGING THOUGHTS ABOUT TEACHING MATHEMATICS TO LOW ATTAINERS.*

I have chosen the above title to be the subject of my study because I know that unless my thinking about mathematics teaching had been changed – unless I had been personally convinced – there could have been no attendant changes in my classroom practice. That is, without a revolution in my philosophy of teaching mathematics, none of the changes which I am now trying to effect in my classroom teaching could have ever come about.

Furthermore, it is because these new approaches in my helping low attainers understand mathematics are firmly grounded in personal conviction that I feel they will stand the test of time.

If I had merely tried out new methods upon somebody else's recommendation, then in the face of difficulty it would be highly probable that I would just 'drop' the ideas. As it is, I sometimes do experience difficulties, and no doubt will in the future, but I know that my underlying convictions will help carry me along."

The teacher had met similar ideas at college several years previously, but had not tried to implement these in the classroom until recently. She had read the Cockcroft Report but had only focused her attention on the Foundation List. She is now developing strategies where pupils can become more confident and involved in their mathematics. The inherent difficulties that she would previously have cited as reasons for not changing are now viewed by her as small hurdles to be negotiated in the course of creating a more worthwhile learning experience for her pupils.

The change in this teacher's behaviour has followed from a change in her convictions.

The power of convictions in shaping behaviour is strong. For instance, teachers who believe that children like and need the security of being told what to do would find it very difficult to put their pupils into a situation where they had to decide what to do for themselves.

The quotes below are from teachers writing about their beliefs:

"The teacher's role is to pass on knowledge."

"Mathematics is not a hierarchical subject – there are many pathways to learning."

"Pupils will only develop mathematically if they are given opportunities to control their own learning."

"The teacher's role should be one of fellow learner."

"Children like and need the security of being told what to do."

"Mathematics must be taught in a logical order. If pupils do not know how to do the basics they cannot progress further."

"An examination syllabus should not be used as a teaching syllabus."

"Exam results are the most important factor."

Through the work of the Project it has become clear that among teachers' sets of beliefs there are a number of 'dominant' convictions which play a major role in determining behaviour. These beliefs centre around two issues:

A. The perception of the nature of mathematics:

'Please Miss, can we do some real maths now?'

It is often the case that teachers have never had the opportunity to examine and sharpen their beliefs in this area, and consequently they and their pupils do not see thinking, questioning, and decision making as integral parts of mathematics.

B. The nature of learning:

'We've done it five times already this year and they still don't understand it.'

Beliefs about how children learn are crucial to actions taken by teachers in the classroom.

*These two areas are considered in greater depth in Chapter 2 – 'Children Learning Mathematics'.*

Dominant beliefs dictate to what extent new ideas will be accepted. When there are strong social pressures to conform, new ideas will be interpreted to fit in with a teacher's existing set of beliefs.

"Right, now we're going to do an investigation, so write this down:
x frogs on the left, x frogs on the right. It takes $x(x+2)$ jumps for frogs to exchange places.
Substitute the numbers 1 to 10 for x and write down your results . . . quietly!"

RICKWOOD 87

STATEMENT 11
If attempts to bring about changes in mathematics teaching rely solely on, for example, adopting new schemes or changing examination syllabuses, then even though the material teachers are using in the classroom may be different, their approach will be essentially the same. Hence, if changes in teachers' behaviour are to be brought about, the teachers themselves must be involved in challenging their beliefs and assumptions.

Teacher development is a complex, individual learning process and as such needs to be embedded in experience.

> **STATEMENT 12**
> **Teachers are education's best resource. All teachers can become more confident and effective in the classroom. No effective far reaching curriculum development can take place without teacher development.**

The Project has identified five generalisations that can be made with regard to helping teachers examine their beliefs critically:

## 1. An element of challenge and risk is essential.

A teacher wrote:

"The first few months have enabled me to think seriously and deeply about my approach to the subject. It has made me question every aspect of my teaching, including things that I thought I was doing well! Psychologically this has been quite traumatic; but essential. Towards the end of this 'shake down' period it has enabled me to experiment confidently, often using the experience and success of other teachers as encouragement."

If teachers are to reach the point where they feel confident enough not only to experiment but also to face failure and learn from it, then it is essential that the initial floundering that is a part of any challenge is not smoothed over in an attempt to 'help'. The ability to face and use dilemmas productively should be highly valued as an objective. It is vital that the right kind of support be available to teachers so that the element of challenge does not become destructive. Strategies for this kind of support are outlined later in this chapter.

## 2. Working in isolation inhibits sustained change.

The most effective support comes from other teachers who are having similar experiences:

"I need to feel that other teachers are suffering from the same pressures as myself. It is useful simply to be able to talk, exchange ideas and renew enthusiasm which inevitably wanes when you feel you are on your own. Whether they succeeded or failed, such experiences are useful in forming one's own 'plan of attack'."

Changes in approach have been best stimulated when groups of teachers have come together to share ideas, compare classroom strategies, and engage in some mathematics. Colleagues discussing and working together on common problems has helped, not only to remove the feeling of isolation, but also to promote greater insight into pupils' learning of mathematics. The value of shared experiences has been evident also where teachers have begun to work with each other in their classrooms. Cooperative teaching has often proved a particularly powerful stimulus for facilitating change. One teacher wrote:

"All too often people will look at pupils' work from other teachers and conclude 'Mine could never do that'. This cooperative teaching has been an opportunity for teachers to see their *own* pupils not only enjoying and getting involved with their mathematics but also producing work that they never thought they could. This is, to my mind, the most significant spur for change anyone could have."

**3.** **Teachers must evolve their own strategies for successful action in their individual classrooms.**

When teachers face difficulties, or are searching for new strategies, they often look for and are given 'solutions' by advisory staff, college lecturers and others who are deemed 'expert'. These agencies must act as catalysts in order to stimulate and facilitate professional development. It is only when teachers are given time to reflect on their experiences and come up with their own solutions and strategies that change becomes lasting and self-sustained. Teachers are often not given credit for the personal resources they have, and therefore undervalue their own experiences.

> **STATEMENT 13**
> The recognition that expertise lies in teachers' own experiences is fundamental to the developmental process.

The following is an extract from an account of a recent in-service course:

"The teachers arrived for their second session, having tried out some mathematical activities with their classes that they had worked on together at the previous session some weeks before. After discussing their classroom trials they generated a list of problems and then began to pool suggestions for 'solving' the problems they had raised. It is interesting that some suggestions were seemingly contradictory, but it became clear to the group that the exercise was not about finding *the answer*, but about pooling experiences and hence increasing their range of classroom strategies. The following are a selection of their problems and 'solutions':

(i) Practical activities are considered 'babyish' by pupils, parents and other teachers. What do I do about this?

First of all, are *you* convinced that they are not 'babyish'? Secondly are *you* convinced that these activities are mathematical? If not do some for yourselves with your colleagues and talk about them. Try offering the activities to 'bright' pupils. Try talking to your pupils about your experiences of working on these activities with other adults and older/ brighter pupils. This gives them credibility and status. Try showing textbooks and exam papers to confirm to the pupils that the activities they do are 'respectable'. If as a result of the activity they can be shown that they can then do 'Exercise C', you are on to a winner.

(ii) Investigative and practical work might not allow pupils to improve their score on tests nor their performance in exams. Should I carry on regardless?

Try and see. Often the key to success in any test is confidence. If the activity you offer increases pupils' confidence it can only help. If what you offer and what you test are very different, do question the effectiveness of your tests as well. The GCSE exam requires pupils to engage in practical, investigative and oral work.

(iii) Pupils may have done the problem but be unable to verbalise their processes. How can I help?

Are you sure they can't verbalise? They might be used to a right/wrong answer atmosphere and might lack the confidence to offer explanations in other contexts. It takes a long time for pupils to trust you when you invite *their* views, and often they feel they still have to play 'guess what's in teacher's mind' games. If pupils have succeeded at a task and enjoyed it they will want to share it with others and talk about it. Engineer situations which will allow them to do this. That might often mean leaving them to talk with other pupils."

## 4. All teachers must be involved in jointly developing schemes of work, assessment models etc.

A visitor to a weekend conference wrote:

"It gave me an insight into a way of teachers working together, an in-service model I have never heard of let alone experienced before. A common view is that teachers have little to offer but much to learn. I have seen that if someone is valued and given credibility they are then able to offer a great deal. This takes longer than arranging a 'tutor-directed' in-service course but is probably more effective."

Efforts to improve mathematics teaching often centre on giving teachers 'props' to help them understand and carry out innovations. These may take the form of 'checklists', simplistic guidelines, external assessment models, schemes or organisational systems. These stand little chance of succeeding if teachers are not involved in either their evolution or in working at the implications affecting their own situation. We have found that when teachers do work together on issues previously thought to be outside their responsibility, such as the final assessment of their pupils' work, they not only become more capable and confident of their own abilities but also more willing to take on these responsibilities.

*This issue is considered further in Chapter 3 – 'Aims and Actions', Chapter 6 – 'Schemes' and Chapter 8 – 'Evaluating and Assessing Mathematics'.*

## 5. Effective change will take time and effort. There are no short cuts.

Often 'props' are given to teachers with the expectation that this will speed up the developmental process. As sustained change can only come about through a change in teachers' attitudes, this is both unrealistic and damaging as it is likely to prevent effective teacher development. Time must be allowed for teachers to become fully involved. The close examination of one's professional performance needs enormous commitment and the time is needed for reflection, discussion and building of confidence. No matter how attractive it may seem, smoothing over these difficulties in the hope of achieving more rapid success is futile.

> **STATEMENT 14**
> **If sustained change is to be effected, it is urgently necessary to explore ways of making time available for teachers to work together as part of a regular pattern of in-service provison. However, to provide time without paying adequate attention to the quality of the in-service experience, as outlined in this chapter, is of no value.**

In all the above five points there are clear parallels between learning activities for children and in-service provision for teachers. Pupils need time for discussion and time for reflection. They need to take responsibility for their own learning and for developing their own strategies. They require challenge, need to be able to make mistakes and to go down blind alleys without feeling a failure. Their mathematical development follows no predetermined regular pattern, and they are capable of becoming far more confident and effective in the subject. These parallels can easily be overlooked by in-service providers.

As teachers are usually successful individuals who have had little experience of academic difficulty, they may understand pupils' feelings and difficulties better when they have been through a similar experience themselves. A teacher on a diploma course commented:

"I was surrounded by more able mathematicians and I knew that some of the tutors were aware of the initial problems I was experiencing. However, during the second term the situation began to improve and I settled down and grew in confidence. I must say that this experience in itself has been invaluable as a teacher. I have become much more aware and sympathetic to problems having experienced the feelings of inadequacy myself."

This has implications for all those involved in educational provision whatever their function. Everyone can benefit from the direct experience of being in a learning situation.

If teachers are to become more confident and effective in the classroom by the means indicated in this chapter, then it is essential that in-service providers believe that teachers are capable of developing their own strategies and evaluating their own and their pupils' work. In the same way that teachers' dominant beliefs determine their behaviour, beliefs about the capabilities of teachers directly determine the mode of, and provision for, in-service work. For example, if in-service providers believe that it is only 'exceptional' teachers who can manage without 'props', then they will not put teachers they consider 'ordinary' into the position where they have to devise their own strategies. A teacher–researcher wrote:

"Having worked regularly with a group of teachers over a period of a few months, I was surprised and a little worried to have what I was doing in my school dismissed on the grounds that I was a 'special' teacher, and that 'ordinary' teachers would not be able to cope with or effect such change.

I reflected on this accusation, and came to the conclusion that the only thing that was special about me was the fact that I had had the opportunity and time to work with other teachers on practical classroom issues. Through this involvement we have all become more honest and articulate about our successes and failures, and it appears we are now deemed 'special'.

It amused and worried me that this incident has a direct parallel with those teachers who dismiss successful work done by pupils in bottom sets by claiming – 'My low attainers are worse than your low attainers'."

If in-service providers are inhibiting teacher development by providing 'props' and 'solutions' then how can they and others play a facilitating role? Some strategies which are proving successful are listed below:

- enabling contacts to be made between teachers from different schools, groups and Local Education Authorities;

- acting as catalysts in order to ensure that professional development of the kind indicated in this chapter is stimulated, supported and sustained;

- helping teachers to set up their own groups and aiding in the administration;

- using advisory teams in a fully supportive role. Imposing them as 'model' demonstration teachers has proved unhelpful and often counter-productive;

- facilitating collaborative teaching and curriculum development generally, on a regular basis through imaginative and flexible timetabling;

- recognising the need for teachers to be allowed time to experiment with ideas obtained on courses. Putting pressure on these teachers to report back in an official capacity or present them as 'expert' has been counter-productive;

- achieving teacher release through extra staffing and ensuring continuity is provided for the pupils. This is best done by incorporating these extra teachers into the staffing of a school rather than employing them on an occasional ad hoc basis.

*In Chapter 5 – 'Widespread, Sustained Curriculum Development' the issues of support groups and networks are explored.*

## The situation

1. Teachers are education's best resource and are capable of becoming more confident and effective in the classroom.

2. Teachers are not given credit for the personal resources they have, and therefore undervalue their own experiences.

3. Convictions shape consistent behaviour. If attempts to bring about change rely solely on changing schemes or examinations, then even though the material a teacher uses in the classroom may be different, their approach to mathematics teaching and learning will remain essentially the same.

4. Solutions and strategies for successful classroom action lie within teachers' own experiences.

5. For many, teaching is an isolating job and working in isolation inhibits sustained change.

6. 'Props' such as checklists, simplistic guidelines, external assessment models, schemes and organisational systems, though well intentioned, are likely to inhibit teacher development.

## Recommendations

1. Effective change will take time and effort. Ways of making time available for teachers to work together need to be explored urgently as part of a regular pattern of in-service provision. However, to provide time without paying adequate attention to the quality of the in-service experience is of no value.

2. In-service providers must act as 'catalysts' in order to ensure that this regular professional development is stimulated and facilitated. Teachers must be actively involved in this process in order to develop their confidence, motivation, autonomy and professionalism both in providing for their pupils' needs and in terms of their own mathematics.

3. This professional development must be recognised as a long term and continuous process. Short cuts are a false economy.

4. In this chapter the Project has identified elements which must form essential parts of teachers' professional development. They have implications for all those involved with in-service provision.

5. If changes in teachers' behaviour are to be facilitated, teachers must be involved in challenging and critically examining their own beliefs.

6. In-service providers must believe that teachers are capable of developing in the ways we have indicated. Hence, they too must be involved in challenging and critically examining their own beliefs.

7. It is essential to recognise that expertise lies in teachers' own experiences. This is fundamental to the developmental process.

8. In-service providers must not be tempted to smooth over the uncertainties and challenges that are an inherent and essential part of teacher development. The ability to face and use dilemmas productively should be highly valued as an objective.

# 5

# WIDESPREAD, SUSTAINED CURRICULUM DEVELOPMENT

A teacher wrote:

"The project I was involved with was envisaged as a teacher supportive, unit based primary scheme conceived in response to criticisms at that time. Its philosophical and organisational basis was exhaustively constructed by a group of practising teachers.

I was involved from the start, making new friends in local schools and meeting the advisory staff at my own and at others' schools. A support group had been formed and trial schools, of which we were one, had a commitment to feed back comments and results to the teacher-writers, either personally or through the advisory team.

It worked well to start with – teachers were less reticent than usual about their experiences, and wrote copiously in order that the units could be improved.

However, under pressures from the publishers, the county advisory staff now changed their attitudes to in-service provision, their position on who should write the material, what sort of trials it should receive, and even the format of the finished material. The pressure to publish forced them to short-circuit the patterns of development outlined above.

The rush to print led them to produce more and more material themselves, or to commission it from college personnel or from the new advisory teachers or from secondary teachers, for use in the primary sector.

The feedback sessions fell into acrimony, the number of courses led by teachers diminished, the coordinators' courses were cancelled, and problems that teachers said they were having with the material were treated as attacks on the scheme itself. The scheme was seen as a monolithic structure, providing all that a child's development required. 'Ordinary' teachers' responses and suggestions were ignored."

This chapter is concerned with curriculum development that aims to improve action in the classroom on a widespread and sustained basis. Such curriculum development is at present not accepted as part of every teacher's responsibility. Although it is considered acceptable and even expected that teachers should evaluate, assess and amend organisational structures such as schemes, setting or mixed ability, they are often not considered by themselves or others to be capable of acting as authorities on the fundamental issue of children's learning. This is left to 'professional researchers' and 'academics'. It is indicative of this situation that practising teachers do not often read educational journals or research findings, seeing in them little relevance to their own experiences. There needs to be recognition that curriculum development and research are essential parts of the teacher's role.

"Job interview?"

RICKWOOD 87

**STATEMENT 15**
Teaching is a researching activity. It is not
desirable to disconnect the two functions.
Isolation and detachment have their place
in the type of enquiry that aims to
accumulate knowledge. However, if the
enquiry aims to improve action in the
mathematics classroom then such isolation
and detachment will bring failure.

We have identified that where initially successful curriculum development has failed
to become widespread, it is because of a 'detachment' – a cut off from the original
source of inspiration. Section A of this chapter (below) concerns the reasons why
detachment occurs, and Section B (pages 44–46) outlines some strategies for avoiding
such detachment.

## SECTION A  REASONS FOR DETACHMENT

**1. Detachment where the curriculum developers/theorists/researchers are
removed from the classroom.**

In some cases developments aimed at improving actions in classrooms seem doomed
from the outset when those involved have never been classroom teachers themselves.
This lack of direct experience and detachment from teachers' problems often leads to
efforts being misdirected in the first place.

In other cases it is classroom teachers who are removed, usually promoted, in order to
engage in curriculum development. Even with direct classroom experience behind
them, this detachment can lead to problems. There is a danger of their perceptions
about the job of teaching becoming 'romanticised'. Memories of day to day pressures
of school life such as writing reports or difficult classes are not as sharp, even after a
short period of absence.

This problem is evident even with respect to in-service models. A college lecturer who
for four years had run an in-service diploma course for experienced teachers was
concerned about the effectiveness of a full-time one-term release pattern as compared
to a one-day-a-week release model:

"Although on the one term course there
are advantages for teachers in not having to
worry about the school organisation and
hence immerse themselves in the course,
there were a number of difficulties. It was
easy to forget some of the circumstances in
which the classroom problems occurred,
and hence the solutions teachers found to
these problems on the course were not
always effective. There were also problems
about 'rehabilitation' after the term's
absence.

The one day a week model, with two one
week residential elements fulfils more
effectively the main aim of the course in
enabling teachers to develop and improve
their craft of teaching. This is because they
can teach and reflect at the same time. The
opportunities for trying out ideas in the
classroom, observing and discussing these

with other teachers, modifying approaches
and then re-testing them regularly, enables
growth of confidence, awareness and
competence. With the one day a week
model this 'active reflection' becomes so
much a part of a teacher's practice, that
there is a greater chance of it continuing
after the end of the course on a sustained
basis, especially when local support groups
play a role.

This model also has the advantage of
allowing teachers to work and
communicate with their school colleagues
without developing a detached language or
status. On the full-time course this is not
always possible and it causes some of the
rehabilitation problems mentioned above.
I have also noticed that the one-day-a-week
course leads to much greater departmental
involvement in teachers' schools."

There is also a danger of a cultural gap developing between practising teachers and those who have been promoted to curriculum development posts. Teachers often become suspicious and cynical about these new 'experts' and because of the teacher's past experiences of such developments the researcher's position loses credibility. It is seen as a way out from the drudgery of working with 'real things', a way to attain status, more money and better working conditions. These aspects often detract from the educational value of a development.

Where any group or individual attempts a curriculum development project there is always the danger of a 'club' mentality forming. An 'in-language' and complacency can set in, leading to an inability and even an unwillingness to communicate with anyone else, or on anything but their own terms. It is essential that communication is two-way and is based on the sharing of common experiences.

## 2. Detachment where the curriculum development begins in the classroom with practising teachers but becomes detached in the dissemination process.

A head of department wrote:

"I find it frustrating when I come across a number of teaching projects in final boxed forms without any indication of the thinking, experimenting, selecting, trials and testing which went on during the writing of these projects.

Another thing that worries me about teaching projects is that most have been written as short term remedies and yet they seem to be presented and used as if they are there to survive forever.

What should be built into projects, either to equip them for long term survival or to point out their short term nature? The latter would be difficult to achieve because vast resources are invested in many projects and regarding them as short term would not justify these investments."

It is often the case that curriculum development projects are conceived in order to tackle specific problems like mixed ability groupings, investigational and practical activities, coherence or individualised work. These are usually carried out by groups of interested, committed and enthusiastic teachers. The development involves these teachers in discussion, reflection, classroom experimentation, evaluation and modification. This personal involvement almost invariably leads to successful outcomes in terms of pupils' motivation, enjoyment and attainment. The problems begin with the attempt to achieve widespread dissemination. It is quite natural that these groups of individuals wish to share their success with others. Invariably, though, it is the 'end point' that the group disseminates. In reality the success of their ventures depended upon their personal active involvement. The wrong thing is disseminated – the material rather than the experience.

Often the in-service work associated with widespread dissemination focuses only on clear explanations of how to use material. Whereas such developments might be locally successful in well motivated departments, these stand little chance of achieving national curriculum change because they become detached from the original source of inspiration. *See Chapter 6 – 'Schemes'.*

External pressures from publishers, Local Education Authorities and central government can contribute to the feeling that the end point or product is more important than the developmental aspects of a project. The offer of publication can be seductive to teachers, but the involvement of these external agencies can often dictate the pace, nature and integrity of a development, as is illustrated by the teacher writing at the beginning of this chapter.

This change of emphasis becomes even more exaggerated when the materials become a commercial success. A teacher concerned about the apparently unforeseen effects of such developments wrote:

"In the late 1950s a similar climate existed in maths education to that which we now experience. There was a strong pressure for change in maths curricula from the OEEC *(Organisation for European Economic Cooperation)*, through the Royaumont Conference of 1959 and within England from pressure groups.

They pushed for change – talked about much the same things which we want now – and PUBLISHED TEXTS. For the people involved in the preparation of these texts – SMP, MME, St. Dunstan's etc. – the process was lengthy and laborious and involved major changes in things other than content – the Preludes in SMP for example.

However, these texts were seized on as a quick way to get 'up to date' and to change what existed by many schools. If you taught from the texts you must be okay. Change could be implemented easily by learning a few new tricks yourself – (Sets, Matrices, Transformations) and then teaching them in the same old way. The consequences are obvious in the CSE type of question on Matrix multiplication.

Apparently quick and easy solutions are not going to work."

Failure to invest in a more complete involvement of teachers can give rise to the myth that not all teachers are capable of understanding the rationale and philosophy behind a development. Further, this lack of involvement can lead to the outright rejection of materials by teachers or to its misuse.

**STATEMENT 18**
**No imported curriculum development exercise can be effective without working commitment and teacher involvement.**

Our own experience has shown us the dangers of people taking on material in good faith, not having had any personal involvement in its development or use. For example, an eager advisory teacher concerned to disseminate what she saw as excellent LAMP Project ideas took some draft in-service material, reproduced it in reduced form and prepared to send it out to all schools in the area. The material was designed to be used in an interactive manner to stimulate and focus discussion and classroom experimentation. The advisory teacher seemed surprised that the material was badly received!

The detachment of teachers from the original aims and purposes of a development can lead them to take up only its more obvious aspects. These often take the form of large organisational systems. Although these may improve attitudes and social change, they may not enhance mathematical development. In this way a teaching system, scheme of workcards, booklets or textbooks can become an end in itself. This account is from a teacher who visited a school with such a system:

"In every classroom I went into, the style of pupil working and the attitudes of pupils and staff to the mathematics going on was similar. The pupils worked on their own, and even the first years were familiar with their system. Comments took the form:

'Who's got the answer book?'

'Oh, I did that card last week, the answer's . . .'

'Who's got card no . . .?'

'How many more have you got to do before you finish your matrix?'

'Aren't you on the test yet?'

'Sir, have you worked out my next matrix?'

I asked many pupils what they thought of the work, but only got comments about the scheme and its organisation:

'I like getting on to the next card.'

'It would be better if there were more answer books.'

I tried to focus more on the mathematics by asking them to talk about what they were doing. In general they spoke without much confidence or conviction. A few did seem intrigued by some aspect of their work, but when I tried to provoke them into asking their own questions about it they politely said they would prefer just to finish it so that they could tick it off and get on to the next card.

The teachers explained their role – they had to decide which cards a pupil should do next helped by a vast network provided for them by the scheme, and of course help when the pupils are stuck. They explained that even though the system is hard to set up, once there it made their life a lot easier.

I left the school depressed, and sat down to analyse why. It came down to the fact that I had seen little mathematics. The pupils rarely worked in groups and therefore had no real opportunity to talk to each other about their work. Even the discussions I had had with pupils and staff had focused almost entirely around 'the system'. Although many of the pupils were enjoying their work and were secure about where they were in the scheme, and although the teachers were secure and comfortable too, the mathematical activity going on in the classrooms seemed superficial.

I began to think about those who had been involved at first hand in creating the scheme. I was sure that their classrooms would be different. What was it that had happened or not happened in the transfer?

I still like the material, I still like some of the philosophy, and I am sure that my 'snapshot' view of the system at work may not be representative. I am also sure, however, that I had seen an organisation that had in some respects 'taken over' and had left pupils with a view of mathematics where the important thing was to get onto the next card and which prompted them when asked what they did yesterday to reply 'Card H.45'."

*Further issues relating to schemes are examined in Chapter 6 – 'Schemes'.*

## SECTION B    AVOIDING DETACHMENT

What dissemination strategies need to be employed in order to avoid detachment?

A teacher on a weekend conference observed:

"The Project has been going for a few years now and much effective change has taken place. That change has not taken place quickly. Each teacher has developed in his/her own way and from that has come the effectiveness and longevity of the Project. The Project is not the original group of teacher–researchers – it is every one of us – and it is our effectiveness and strength that brings the change.

Learning from our weaknesses enables us to develop further. Through our learning and growing the Project extends and encompasses more people. But it takes a long time to change.

The Project is supportive during this frustrating time, because the Project is people. We help each other in many ways so the changing and adjusting goes on, taking more time, more effort, each person supporting others who then support others, who then support others . . .

There are no short cuts. Would we, as caring teachers, try to stunt a child's growth of confidence by always giving him/her our short cuts when they are working on a piece of mathematics? We might assist by helping, supporting, but not by taking short cuts or trying to find easy answers.

We must look on our development as an ongoing thing. Once we think we've got there we stop developing."

**STATEMENT 19**
**To succeed on a wider scale, dissemination must be firmly rooted in the personal experiences of teachers in their classrooms. Hence it must depend on personal contact based on shared experience. This can only be achieved through involving more and more teachers in active support networks.**

Within the six Local Education Authorities involved with LAMP we have already seen the power of such contact in the form of teacher support groups as well as more specific 'task' oriented teacher working groups concerned with issues such as assessment, parents and industry. These groups are all very different. They started up in a variety of ways, their meetings have different formats, they have different emphases and they give rise to other groups. The LAMP network groups are not isolated. The focus provided by the Project has enabled connections to be made between the various groups. They draw and feed from each other, and together they form a powerful and ever growing support network. The fact that the groups once initiated have been largely self-sustaining, have flourished and continued to grow throughout the period of the Project (1983–6) illustrates the importance attached to them by teachers. Attempts to generate such a network *for* teachers by imposing a structure of formally constituted groups is unlikely to succeed, as this support-group member indicates:

"The formalities and career-linked high profile leadership of imposed groups would be totally different in character to the informality and low profile 'leadership' of the original teacher initiated groups. Moves from the top may lead to these groups being formally set up by LEAs or others with the result that the original groups disappear."

The organic nature of the Project network ensures that the type of detachment described earlier can never occur. Its growth depends on the teachers within it. They feel they want to share their successes, but they are not disseminating a set of materials, nor even a set of ideas. They are, instead, involving more and more teachers in a way of working together that enables them to develop their own strategies and hence become more confident and competent in their classrooms. Dissemination of this kind is not easy or quick, but it is effective and long lasting because it is firmly rooted in the personal experiences of teachers in their classrooms. Teachers do not view their development as 'a fad' that will disappear along with all the others because their *beliefs* about learning and mathematics have changed.

*Strategies that facilitate the above development are outlined further in Chapter 4 – 'Teacher Development'.*

**STATEMENT 20**
**If curriculum development is to be widespread, successful and sustained, money must be made available to release teachers on a regular basis.**

An adviser visiting a weekend conference wrote:

"My reason for coming was a quest for knowledge and a desire to know how LAMP operated with a view to supporting a similar development in my region.

If the amazing changes in teachers' perception of the 'learning process' had taken place, I wanted to know the secret.

Why were well established and successful teachers totally changing their outlook (for the better) in mid-career? What was the motivation for the change? What was the catalyst for change? How was the development sustained, nurtured and able to grow? I was going to be a sponge, to lap up all the answers – or so I thought.

Well it didn't happen quite like that. I don't know all the answers (possibly no one does), but I can now see the operating strategy.

I have enjoyed the 'involvement' of the weekend – a chance to discuss and sharpen arguments – to indulge in some mathematical activity. The emphasis on reflection has been valuable. Writing down thoughts has proved to be a difficult but essential activity.

I now have a better view of the LAMP strategy, and it will help me to prepare a case for support and local development. The experience will help me to argue with conviction."

## SUMMARY

### The situation

1. Curriculum development and research are not seen as integral parts of the job of teaching.

2. Teachers are often not considered by themselves or others to be capable of acting as authorities on the matter of children's learning.

3. Where initially successful curriculum development has failed to become widespread, it is because of a 'detachment' – a cut off from the original source of inspiration.

4. Whereas the most important part of any curriculum development is teacher involvement, what is invariably disseminated is only a written product.

5. External pressures have often dictated the pace, nature and integrity of a development thus taking it out of the hands of the original group of teachers.

6. Imported developments are often misused or rejected. No imported curriculum development exercise can be effective without commensurate working commitment and teacher involvement.

7. Present budgeting and organisation allows for only small numbers of teachers to be released per Local Education Authority for the purposes outlined in this and the previous chapter.

8. The focus provided by the Project has facilitated:

   a) the formation of various working groups of teachers;

   b) the continuation of groups after the completion of their initial task or course;

   c) connections between the various groups hence maximising their impact.

### Recommendations

1. There needs to be recognition that curriculum development and research are essential parts of the teacher's role.

2. In order to achieve widespread, successful and sustained curriculum development, teachers must be allowed time on a regular basis and financial and organisational support must be provided.

3. If curriculum change is to be widespread and sustained, it is essential that developments do not remain focused around a small group of apparently successful and enthusiastic individuals.

4. To succeed on a wider scale, dissemination must be firmly rooted in the personal experiences of teachers in their classrooms. It must depend upon a cellular growth of working groups based on personal contact, rather than on a written product. This can only be achieved through involving more and more teachers in active support networks.

# 6

# SCHEMES

On an in-service course, a head of department wrote of her anxieties to an imagined publisher:

"Dear Publisher,

Over the last three years I have been working at changing my teaching but the biggest stumbling block has been trying to 'break out' of a textbook centred approach.

It is difficult not to panic about 'whether we will cover the syllabus'. This is particularly difficult when trying to encourage other colleagues to change and they have read the claims of publishers such as 'takes on board all the Cockcroft principles', 'lively and interesting approach to stimulate low attaining pupils' etc. When you actually look inside these books they still seem dull, stereotyped and concentrated solely on skills practice.

At exhibitions you tell us that the formal skills practice books are still the best sellers so you could not think of publishing practising teachers' 'real' ideas.

PLEASE get more involved with what we are trying to do and regard your part in the education process as supportive rather than simply commercial."

In responding to such calls many publishers and authors claim they are indeed providing facilitating material. Typical publishers' claims are below:

*'We provide a structured course that when followed ensures a sense of progression, and from which nothing is left out.'*

*'The scheme helps probationers and non-specialists.'*

*'The scheme involves a use of equipment.'*

*'The scheme enables pupils to get on at their own pace.'*

*'The subject is broken down into easily digestible topics.'*

*'The scheme has easy to operate inbuilt assessment and record keeping devices.'*

*'The scheme ensures that pupils meet mathematics in real life situations.'*

This chapter is concerned with published schemes (below), home-made schemes (page 51) and the use of resources (page 53).

## SECTION A    PUBLISHED SCHEMES

We have found cause for concern in the adverse effects that a close adherence to a published scheme can have on both children's learning of mathematics and teachers' professional development. Seven of these concerns are outlined below.

1. Investigatory or enquiry elements of schemes are often left out by teachers, frequently because of 'syllabus pressures'. This is an age old problem which can be easily exemplified from most post-war publications. In trying to resolve this some schemes have attempted to include enquiry as a compulsory component of their course. However, there are two problems with this.

   (i) Because the more stretching investigatory elements of some schemes are not reached until initial material has been completed by pupils, it is often only the quicker children who get a taste of this kind of work. *All* children need and benefit from mathematical exploration. (*See Chapter 2 – 'Children Learning Mathematics'.*)

   (ii) When given greater status, and often in order to 'help' the teacher, investigatory elements can become prescriptive and limiting, precluding the teachers' and children's own questions and losing all sense of real enquiry or exploration. The following writing illustrates this concern:

"What is it that some schemes offer pupils when they include their 'Investigations' chapter or booklet? All too often these consist of a long list of questions beautifully annotated and carefully structured so ensuring that pupils will be able to work independently and have enough to get on with, but offer no encouragement to ask questions of their own.

If all the questions come from text, worksheet, blackboard or are asked by me then what is the essence within the mathematical experience undergone by my pupils that warrants my calling it an investigation?

The word is becoming devalued – perhaps we should avoid it."

2.  New schemes are often chosen because they are seen to cater for a particular organisational classroom priority. However, the 'prices' that are paid for these priorities may well have adverse effects on the children's mathematical experiences. For example if the priority is to ensure that pupils can 'get on' independently of their teacher, there is a danger that a scheme which provides for this may also lead to the mathematical content being unnaturally fragmented. *(See Chapter 2 – 'Aims and Actions' and Chapter 5 – 'Widespread, Sustained Curriculum Development'.)*

3.  By their nature most schemes are answer-oriented, some to make life easier for teachers, some to encourage pupils to 'work back' from solutions and some to enable pupils to mark their own work so as not to hamper their speed of progression. One teacher writes of the answer-oriented view his scheme has given his pupils:

"As work is self-marked, only questions with a single answer are asked . . . but some of the cards do say 'what do you notice?' Pupils quickly learn that there is AN answer to this to and either look up answers or ask a teacher, who provides the words.

Responses not in the exact form of words in the answer sheets are marked wrong by pupils. Any teacher intervention in this process, with positive encouragement to speculate, is viewed with suspicion. Authority rests with the answer sheets!"

rst published 1979
. edition, 2nd impression 1980
 edition, 3rd impression 1981
 edition, 4th impression 1982
 edition, 5th impression 1983
 edition, 6th impression 1984

.B.N.  0 834 82903 1 (Pupils)
.B.N.  0 844 82904 X (Answers)

4.  Many mathematics schemes now include microcomputer software packages. There is, however, a danger that computers are not realising their potential as powerful vehicles for mathematical enquiry and development in the classroom. Although many of the programs within the packages can provide excellent starting points for exploration, some are no more than simulations of what are considered to be successful classroom activities. When these activities are 'translated' for use on a computer they sometimes lack flexibility, precluding and limiting opportunities for pupils to follow up their own ideas or organise their own work. All too often the packages in general are used as 'rewards' and devices to 'keep the pupils occupied'.

5.  The teacher's role can be undermined by a close adherence to a polished scheme. A teacher wrote:

"My horror stories are not so much the schemes as the teachers who:

go in knowing that 25th March means p 47 Book 2;

rely on their scheme to prepare their lessons for them;

feel that published schemes know better than they do;

are so bound by the structure of a scheme that they can't, or don't want to try anything else;

think it's the scheme's and examination's job to motivate their pupils;

feel too comfortable to be open minded about change."

Much of the undermining occurs because a scheme is seen to take over classroom responsibilities that should be those of the teacher. Responding to the immediate needs of individual children, controlling material, deciding what should happen next and what pathways of learning should be encouraged are all essential parts of the teacher's role and cannot be generalised by an external system written for unknown children and teachers. The head of department's letter at the beginning of this chapter contains an understandable plea for support. However, in expecting published material to give this kind of support, she is asking for something that cannot be provided externally.

6. Frequently an adherence to a scheme is seen as a necessary support for so-called 'weak teachers'. However, even as a short term solution this can be unsatisfactory and often counter-productive. This is also true of the understandable concern frequently expressed about probationary teachers of mathematics as this head of department indicates:

"If, as I believe, teaching is improved through reflecting on our classroom experiences, then to consider a scheme as something that will 'make it OK for a probationary teacher' is arrant nonsense, since it denies the ways in which teachers develop their abilities.

Most schemes, by APPEARING to make a probationary an effective teacher – ie able to keep the class 'happy' and 'occupied at their tasks' can undermine that teacher's development, hiding the real need for it. That is a most pernicious effect.

Schemes need to be 'patchy' in order that the teacher has to take responsibility for the development in children of the processes and strategies of mathematical activity."

For all teachers, support and development of the kind indicated throughout this report are essential.

A considerable part of the teaching of mathematics is done by non-specialists. These are sometimes strong teachers of their first subject, and it is commonly assumed that they will benefit from even more guidelines and will need a strictly prescriptive mathematics scheme. We have found, however, that the development of these teachers is also undermined by such a provision. When allowed the time for an element of 'retraining' that embodies the features outlined in Chapter 4 – 'Teacher Development', their development is also facilitated and they can become significant members of a mathematics department, bringing unique insights and making valuable contributions. A tutor on such a retraining course wrote:

"It was interesting to see that teachers arrived with a very limited idea of mathematics and mathematics teaching.

Having been given the opportunity on the course to engage in mathematics themselves in an exploratory and creative way, and thus experience the positive aspects of the subject, they began to realise their own capabilities in mathematics.

This experience also enabled them to see how successful teaching approaches from their own subject area could be used in this new area of the curriculum.

One teacher told me about how she taught English, describing how she collected materials, utilised the pupils own ideas and generally fuelled their creativity. The realisation slowly dawned on her that she could teach mathematics in the same way."

**STATEMENT 21**
**Schemes are offered in good faith by advisers, headteachers and other concerned agencies to teachers of mathematics as 'solutions' to classroom problems. In practice, because in the end schemes fundamentally undermine the principles of teacher development, they become major inhibitors to improvement in the quality of mathematics teaching.**

7. New schemes are often taken on in order to initiate change in static teaching situations dominated by exposition and textbooks. Sometimes this is in order to respond to a national initiative such as the recommendations of the Cockcroft Committee, or GCSE. We have found that where a department is aware that the new scheme is merely a starting point for discussion and development it has been beneficial. However, in many cases even when schemes have been taken on in this spirit they have failed to facilitate development. Key teachers leave, financial investment inhibits rejection and busy teachers with other responsibilities who would have been in a strong position to contribute to departmental development become reluctant to endanger what is for them a familiar, administratively efficient system. In these all too frequent cases the scheme becomes a substitute for genuine teacher development rather than a vehicle for it, and the quality of the children's mathematics learning may well not be improved. Teachers begin to teach 'the scheme' rather than teach mathematics. *(See Chapter 2 – 'Children Learning Mathematics', Chapter 4 – 'Teacher Development' and Chapter 5 – 'Widespread, Sustained Curriculum Development'.)*

**STATEMENT 22**
**No mathematics scheme alone can meet the needs of pupils and an adherence to any scheme may prove detrimental to their mathematics. The mathematical development of pupils can only be encouraged, sustained, evaluated and assessed by the personal involvement of their teachers. It is not possible to produce a definitive scheme which will apply to all pupils or situations, even within specific ability ranges.**

| **SECTION B** | **HOME-MADE SCHEMES** |

Faced with the above problems, or in efforts to increase departmental involvement, or in order to deal with a school-specific problem (mixed ability, team teaching etc.) many departments decide to produce their own scheme, often based on a prescribed sequence of home-made workcards, booklets or worksheets. We have found that in time there is a real danger of these schemes becoming as habitual as published schemes, and that in many cases the same problems are to be found. Added to these is the strength of attachment that is derived from the expenditure of personal time and effort. This makes change and flexibility that much harder to achieve. A head of department wrote:

"Teachers cannot afford to be sentimental about the form – of organisation, resources, methods etc. – when they accept responsibilities for the mathematical growth of their pupils. They need much greater confidence in themselves so that they can 'kick around' and experiment with new methods and materials. They need to develop their power to live, change, grow and respond so that they can meet changes and disturbances which are present in life. This they can hardly begin to develop if most of their energies and beliefs are invested in methods, organisations and 'materials'."

A teacher who inherited a highly acclaimed home-produced scheme wrote about it while looking at paragraph 243 of the Cockcroft Report:

"The scheme demands that the following happen:

**1. Exposition**
We have 'lead-lessons' for each year group.

**2a. Discussion between teacher and pupil**
This happens in all other lessons, but the scheme does dictate the nature of that discussion; it tends to be 'answer giving', 'how to do it', rather than shared talk.

**2b. Discussion between pupils themselves**
Grouping around tables allows this, but it is used as the worst punishment to make pupils work in silence for a time. Does this mean discussion is a privilege not a necessity?

**3. Appropriate practical work**
Some tasks demand painting, drawing, using dice, pinboards, cutting up paper, making models, but who are these appropriate for? All pupils tackle these activities simultaneously. Have you ever seen 120 children all using glue at the same time? It is terrifying!

**4. Consolidation and practice of fundamental skills and routines**
'Basic skills' are on particular sheets in the first and third year, tackled fortnightly. So if 'basic skills' are 'sums' the scheme has these.

**5. Problem solving**
The nearest the scheme has to this is some sheets which offer a mixture of tricks, jokes and some reasonable 'starters' (with an answer!)

**6. Investigational work**
'Investigations' occur in fourth and fifth year work. 'Find out about . . .' occurs frequently but in practice means 'ask a teacher' or 'look it up'. Several tasks at the end of topic books are headed 'investigation' but (i) few pupils get this far, and (ii) the answers are on the answer sheets.

Certainly, our scheme could be said to satisfy Cockcroft paragraph 243! Is this 'good practice'?"

Home-made schemes, and even departmental schemes of work, are often designed to be as flexible as possible, but without continual re-evaluation and modification involving the *whole* department, a scheme can quickly stagnate and its content take on a higher significance than was meant. A teacher wrote:

"I'm really concerned about the power of the written word. Once something has been formalised it can take on a far greater importance than was perhaps originally intended.

Last summer two teachers put together a 3rd year scheme of work – some of it based upon what they had done with their own groups over the year. It meant very little to me when I first read it. I didn't understand why it was organised the way it was, why the content included particular topics and not others, or why the activities listed had been chosen.

The entire document seemed useless to me. I abandoned it, along with several other teachers in the department, and instead we got together and tried to sort out what we were going to do.

If I'd been involved in the formation of the departmental scheme of work I'd have realised the flexibility that was implicit in its structure."

**STATEMENT 23**
**A scheme cannot be a substitute for an ongoing dialogue with colleagues. This generates more ideas and an increased awareness of pupils' needs. The continuing process of development is more important than the particular details of the curriculum. There are no short cuts and the process takes time.**

*(See Chapter 3 – 'Aims and Actions', Chapter 4 – 'Teacher Development' and Chapter 5 – 'Widespread, Sustained Curriculum Development'.)*

# SECTION C    USING RESOURCES

A teacher described an incident with a bottom set, second year class:

"Two girls came up to me and asked if they could do some 'sums'. They were fed up with what they were doing. I had some very old textbooks in a cupboard that were full of exercises containing dozens of 'sums' ranging from the four rules to quadratic equations. They were meant as practice for pupils of considerably higher age and ability than these girls, but I rather dismissively told them they were there and that they could choose something from them to do if they wanted.

When I got back to them they were happily engaged in experimenting with their calculators in order to obtain answers to an exercise entitled 'Changing Vulgar Fractions into Decimals'.

Not only were they not put off by the title but the only piece of sound knowledge they had was that a half equals 0.5. From this piece of information they were successfully completing the exercise."

Pupils in this class were used to asking their own questions about their mathematics and hence when offered material that would seem to be extremely uninviting they accepted it, as they normally would, as a challenge. Their personal motivation was sufficient for them to sustain exploration on their own and achieve good results.

> **STATEMENT 24**
> **When teachers and pupils are accustomed to exploring mathematical ideas and have established a positive attitude to learning, then almost any material can be used as a stimulus for mathematical enquiry in the classroom.**

There is, at present, a wide variety of useful resources available for teachers and pupils in mathematics lessons. These include ideas within existing schemes and textbooks, resources in the form of thematic and topic booklets, books and periodicals containing ideas and 'starters', catalogues and timetables, reference material, magazine and newspaper articles, games and practical materials including calculators and computers, as well as the resources that the children bring with them to school in terms of ideas, interests and miscellaneous items. Spending limited departmental funds on 'packaged' schemes often means that no money remains for these forms of resources. This has implications in terms of teacher awareness about what is potentially useful in their mathematics classroom, and about what physical accommodation is necessary in order to work at the subject in the ways indicated throughout this report. In the first case we have found that when given the opportunities for teacher development as indicated in Chapter 4, teachers have become more discerning and more demanding consumers of published material and equipment. In the second, it is essential that senior management do not look upon mathematics as a subject that can be taught in any room in the school as long as it has a blackboard and some chalk.

> **STATEMENT 25**
> **It is part of the professional concern of all teachers to take responsibility for choosing appropriate materials which will encourage pupils to learn mathematics. It is this professional responsibility which needs encouragement, time and resources to develop.**

## The situation

1. There is cause for concern about the adverse effects that a close adherence to a published scheme can have on children's learning of mathematics.

2. Investigatory or enquiry elements of schemes are often left out by teachers, frequently because of 'syllabus pressures'.

3. It is often only the quicker children who get a taste of the more stretching investigatory elements of some schemes, because they are not reached until initial material has been completed.

4. In many schemes investigatory elements have become prescriptive and limiting.

5. By their nature most schemes are answer-oriented.

6. Schemes are offered in good faith by advisers, headteachers and other concerned agencies to teachers of mathematics as solutions to classroom problems. In practice, schemes can become major inhibitors to improvements in the quality of mathematics teaching, because ultimately they undermine the principles of teacher development.

7. The mathematical development of pupils can only be encouraged, sustained, evaluated and assessed by the personal involvement of their teachers.

8. No mathematics scheme alone can meet the mathematical needs of pupils.

9. It is not possible to produce a definitive mathematics scheme which will apply to all pupils or situations, even within specific ability ranges.

10. Home-made schemes, if not constantly reviewed, will suffer from the same problems as published schemes.

11. When teachers and pupils are accustomed to exploring mathematical ideas and have established a positive attitude to learning, then almost any material can be used as a stimulus for mathematical enquiry in the classroom.

12. There is, at present, a wide variety of useful resources available for pupils in mathematics lessons.

13. When allowed the opportunities for teacher development as indicated in Chapter 4, teachers have become more discerning and more demanding consumers of published material and equipment.

## Recommendations

1. A scheme must not take over classroom responsibilities such as responding to the immediate needs of individual children, controlling material, deciding what should happen next and what pathways of learning should be encouraged. These responsibilities are those of the teacher and cannot be generalised by an external system.

2. Schemes and schemes of work should be continuously evaluated and modified. This process must include the *whole* department, and is more important than the particular details of the curriculum. There are no short cuts and the process takes time.

3. Resources in the form of ideas, thematic and topic booklets, catalogues and timetables, books and periodicals, reference material, magazine and newspaper articles, games and practical materials including calculators and computers are needed. The spending of limited departmental funds on 'packaged' schemes should be seriously questioned by schools as this often means that no money remains for these other forms of resources and can lead to inflexibility.

4. It is essential that mathematics is recognised as a subject which has special accommodation requirements.

5. It must be seen to be part of the professional concern of all teachers to take responsibility for choosing appropriate materials which will encourage pupils to learn mathematics. It is this professional responsibility which needs encouragement and funds to develop.

# 7

# WORKING ACROSS THE CURRICULUM

A teacher wrote:

> "In my early years of teaching I used to teach Physics and Mathematics, and one year I taught both to the same fourth year group.
>
> I was aware that the Physics department among others used to complain about pupils' inability to manipulate formulae and perform what were regarded as simple and basic mathematical skills in their classes. I had a certain amount of sympathy with these complaints as I too had noticed pupils' inability to apply their mathematics in Physics lessons.
>
> The year I was allocated the same group for Mathematics and Physics I thought I would be in a position to change things for the better since I would be able to use the Mathematics lessons to teach pupils exactly what they needed in Physics. I did.
>
> To my surprise I still found that what most pupils could do confidently in my Maths class, they were not able to transfer into their Physics lessons with me during the same week! What was even more sad was the fact that they failed to appreciate the joke when I told them that they must have an awful Mathematics teacher!"

This problem of lack of transference between disciplines is as old as subject boundaries themselves. Two of the more common strategies designed to deal with the perceived artificiality of subject divisions and to resolve problems of this kind have been of particular concern to us.

## 1. Inter-departmental discussions and meetings.

'Do you think you could teach trig before we teach refraction?'

'Do you really not teach pi until the third year?'

'If they want them to know about it why don't they teach it to them themselves?'

'But we always teach them ratio this way.'

'The Science department say that the first years can't read off the scales on their measuring cylinders, so I said we'd do 'Reading Graphs' as the first topic of the year.'

Frequently inter-departmental meetings are held as responses to perceived external demands. Terms such as 'cross-curricular links', 'inter-disciplinary enquiry', 'integrated curriculum', 'language across the curriculum', 'mathematics across the curriculum', 'life skills' and 'whole school policies' sound plausible but are often tackled only at an administrative level, concentrating purely on content overlap. A head of department commented on his experiences:

> "One thing that leaves me constantly frustrated and dissatisfied is 'cross-curricular' links.
>
> I have read reports and heard advisers, inspectors and others pointing out where links exist with other departments.
>
> I have been involved in meetings where attempts to make the curriculum more 'coherent' have taken place. Mostly these have been in the form of each head of department explaining his or her scheme and syllabus to others and ending up with an ordered list of topics which each department should cover in order that pupils can cope with certain ideas and principles in various subjects without having to be taught these several times.
>
> I have also been aware that these decisions, however well implemented, have had little effect on pupils' ability to transfer their skills across, or see links between other subjects."

## 2. A 'thematic' approach.

The frustrations caused by the apparent artificiality of subject divisions have led to some initiatives abandoning the discipline boundaries completely. Children explore themes such as 'Christmas', 'Water' or 'Railways', or work on community projects. Theoretically subject content should emerge in context through such projects and therefore help pupils to gain an overview of the curriculum and see the relevance of particular techniques and skills. In practice, however, this does not always happen. Because of concern that pupils should get the required quota of 'Geography' or 'Science' out of their project the subject matter can become trivial and contrived, especially as far as mathematics is concerned.

Both in inter-departmental meetings, and in 'thematic' projects of the types described, mathematics is usually seen and discussed only as a 'service subject', especially with regard to 'low attainers'. This reinforces many teachers' and pupils' preconceptions about the nature of mathematics. It is precisely these assumptions that must be tackled if any meaningful cross-curricular work involving mathematics is to be developed. If mathematics is only seen as utilitarian or tied to a theme approach, however practically and relevantly based, then when it is offered in its own right, the subject may be regarded as uninteresting and unimportant. A large part of the mathematical development and experience that we have found essential for *all* pupils will therefore not occur. (*See Chapter 2 – 'Children Learning Mathematics'.*)

A college lecturer wrote:

"Mathematics has a great deal to offer in terms of its potential for creativity, its special use of language and its opportunities for conjecture, proof and modelling. To reduce the richness the mathematics specialist can offer to merely doing your calculations for you is as absurd as asking the English specialist just to correct your spelling, the Geographer to read your map or the P.E. specialist occasionally to lead a run around the block."

**STATEMENT 26**
**If pupils of all abilities are to experience both the richness of individual subjects and gain an overview of the subtle inter-relationships and interactions that exist among disciplines it is essential to maintain *both* the links and the separation between subjects.**

It is not surprising that there are difficulties in achieving these inter-disciplinary relationships when one considers the deep-seated stereotypes that exist within schools.

Why are children always so surprised that their teachers have hobbies and expertise outside their subject area?

A teacher reported:

"As I was passing the boys' changing room I heard the P.E. teacher say to some of *my* mathematics pupils, 'If you don't get changed quickly, you'll be back after school and I'll give you some Maths to do.'"

Overheard in a pastoral head's office:

'Is Geography better now you are sitting next to Tracy?'

'I know you find Maths hard but you really will need it.'

'Are you still finding it hard to get your Science homework done?'

'It's nice to see your History marks have gone up.'

'How are you getting on in English?'

When talking to pupils about subjects other than their own, why do teachers rarely seem to show interest in the actual ideas and subject content involved in those lessons?

A teacher said:

"I came across a second year pupil who didn't know how many days there were in a year. I found myself wondering whose job it was to teach him things like that."

Why do so many teachers feel guilty if one of their lessons ends up by being an interesting digression into another subject area?

Where does a child learn about 3-D space?
In Maths? In CDT? In Geography? In Dance? . . .

In a mathematics lesson on Sets, the children were asked to list all the countries in Europe beginning with a vowel. They couldn't think of many. The mathematics teacher wondered what on earth they did in Geography lessons.

A teacher wrote:

"Our school had some money to spend on library books. The Maths department put in a list of exciting resource books for the librarian to buy. When the library was stocked we went to look for the books. We couldn't find them in the Maths section. We said to the librarian, 'Where are the books we ordered?' We told her the titles. She said, 'Oh I put them in the Recreation and Games section. . .'"

**STATEMENT 27**
**Most of the problems encountered in working across the curriculum are due to, and exacerbated by, the enormous lack of awareness that exists in schools about what everyone else is doing, and about the nature of different subjects. This is especially true of mathematics where strange preconceptions are rife.**

When teachers become more aware of what is going on in other classrooms they are more likely to be able to use that understanding to best effect both in their own subject lessons and in any joint subject initiatives. The climate created by such awareness is a prime factor in breaking down children's stereotypes of teachers' specialist roles. This awareness can only be achieved through teachers working together and being interested in children's experiences in other curriculum areas. Cooperation must develop at teacher level and has major implications for teacher release and staffing. There are numerous opportunities for senior management to play a facilitating role through flexible timetabling and staffing, altered priorities etc., but when initiatives are imposed by management on their staff without those teachers being involved and committed, then such initiatives are unlikely to be sustained.

When new areas are created for children to study which attempt to be cross-curricular in nature, eg TVEI, 'Life Skills', Information Technology or Computer Awareness, there is a danger that without the general awareness described earlier, they will end up by being just another subject slot on the timetable. Those who are not involved will often have little idea of what goes on, thus destroying the spirit behind the initiatives. *(See Chapter 3 – 'Aims and Actions', Chapter 4 – 'Teacher Development' and Chapter 5 – 'Widespread, Sustained Curriculum Development'.)*

# Forging effective cross-curricular links

A teacher wrote:

"It must be possible to peel away the trimmings, ie different resources and specific subject language, to concentrate on pupil learning, in order that the pupils can recognise common approaches and become more actively involved in the learning process."

Over the past three years teachers associated with the Project have managed to forge strong, regular and fruitful links with other subject areas. Because these were developed at teacher level the strategies adopted are all very different according to the opportunities that arose within individual schools. A common feature, however, is that all have recognised the need to open their lessons to other teachers and work together in their classrooms. This is not always easy, as the following teachers indicate:

"Changes across the curriculum will only come from a change in teachers' attitudes towards themselves. Will they have the willingness to open up their classroom doors? Will they have the confidence to admit they don't always know the 'best' way for children to do things?"

"I need to open up my teaching space to others, to invite them in at any time – not just to see the 'good' lessons, but to witness the failures as well, so that we might discuss approaches and methods as yet unexplored."

The writing below is from a mathematics teacher who was interested to see whether a teaching approach that gave pupils more responsibility for their own learning could have the same positive effects in another curriculum area:

"A friendly Geographer had taken up the invitation to come into my lessons and he enjoyed the way the children were working and was keen for me to come into his Geography lessons.

As with the other cross-curricular discussions I had had, it was important to both of us that our cooperation was not at the level of 'When do you teach coordinates and scale?'. We were sure that the most important common ground was our joint concern over how we could help children to learn, increase their motivation, and generally allow them more control over their work.

I found myself being genuinely excited by the diversity and richness of the pupils' ideas, and discussing our notes at the end of the first lesson made us both realise that the pupils' discussion had covered the Geography syllabus for the term. We felt we had to find a way of following up the children's questions and ideas and not simply impose our own onto them.

There followed six weeks of the children working on different aspects of the third world and poverty.

The following elements of our Geography project stood out for me as being necessary components of any learning/teaching situation, and as such transferable across all subject areas:

**Responsibility and challenge** – The pupils were pleased to take on the responsibility and challenge of controlling to a great extent what they did and how they did it. It became their work not ours.

**Starting from where the pupils are** – Because they had to make their own decisions about where and how to start there was no question of 'teaching to the middle of the ability range'.

**Pupils following through and extending their ideas** – In the course of their work many pupils wrote away to various embassies and individuals for information and opinions. The basic ideas were theirs and their satisfaction and pride were evident when they received replies. In this way the pupils began to realise that they did have it in them to find things out, not only independently of their teachers, but also outside their teachers' knowledge.

**Enjoyment** – It is an encouraging sign that when these pupils had to choose their options for the 4th year, many who had previously not considered taking Geography are now doing so. We in Maths do not have to face this ultimate consumer test, but it is interesting to consider what would happen if we did.

I think there are direct parallels here for any subject lesson. The atmosphere was identical to that of my mathematics lessons where for example pupils may be working on an idea of their own to which they and I have no idea of an outcome but share an excitement for both the process of discovery and the expectation of results, positive or negative.

It would now be impossible for us not to wish to continue looking at our teaching approaches and exploring classroom strategies that facilitate pupils to learn, gain in confidence and motivation, develop their thinking and study skills as well as widening their appreciation of the subject matter in hand.''

The sustained nature of this work is evident from the comment of the geography teacher who wrote some time later:

"The initial point that struck me when we started working together was that any innovation is best done with more than one person. Trying new things by yourself is very difficult, exhausting and disheartening.

My overall feelings about the work we have done can be summed up in my feelings towards the group. When I taught them in the second year they were argumentative, restless and lacking in motivation.

This year although they have remained quite noisy they have shown much more interest in the subject. I have been pleased to see how the 'quietest', 'nervous' personalities in the group have gained in confidence.

We obviously do not give pupils enough responsibility and freedom to come up with their own ideas.''

### STATEMENT 28
**Whilst each subject area makes a unique contribution to the curriculum, all share a common concern for the development of pupils' knowledge, skills and attitudes. Changes in teachers' attitudes to learning have considerable implications for individual classrooms and hence have the potential for development across all subjects.**

In Chapter 2 – 'Children Learning Mathematics' we reported on the attempt by a group of teachers to describe the necessary ingredients for a rich mathematical activity (page 20). In the light of the preceding teachers' experiences it is interesting to see how easily one can generalise the list:

### WHAT MAKES A RICH CLASSROOM ACTIVITY?

- **It must be accessible to everyone at the start.**
- **It needs to allow further challenges and be extendible.**
- **It should invite children to make decisions.**
- **It should involve children in speculating, hypothesis making and testing, proving or explaining, reflecting, interpreting.**
- **It should not restrict pupils from searching in other directions.**
- **It should promote discussion and communication.**
- **It should encourage originality/ invention.**
- **It should encourage 'what if' and 'what if not' questions.**
- **It should have an element of surprise.**
- **It should be enjoyable.**

Some teachers were able to obtain release from their normal timetable commitments in order to work in each others' schools, initially in mathematics lessons and then on a broader basis. One teacher writes about the effects of this cooperative work:

"They have introduced a breath of fresh air and enthusiasm – they have opened up a way of promoting communications between different departments. They have made a few of us realise that we are not alone with our ideas and that there are other staff in our school who feel the same way about children and teaching."

Subsequently this teacher was allowed time to work at building on these links within his own school. We have found that where external funds have been utilised for teacher release, a variety of fruitful initiatives have begun. To be of real value, these initiatives must be based on a strong, shared working commitment.

A mathematics teacher wrote about a different strategy he used to begin to break down preconceptions:

"An English teacher joined me with a class on a day's outing to the West Sussex Institute where she, I and the pupils spent a day doing mathematical activities. She found this particularly useful, not just because of the methods and ideas used, but as an insight into her own reactions to being in a learning situation."

**STATEMENT 29**
**If sustained, meaningful cross-curricular links are to be effected, then teachers must be provided with mechanisms to work together on a long term basis.**

This has the same implications for support and provision, both in and out of school, that are outlined in *Chapter 4 – 'Teacher Development' and Chapter 5 – 'Widespread, Sustained Curriculum Development'*.

| SUMMARY | The situation | Recommendations |

**The situation**

1. Lack of transference between curriculum areas is a common problem.

2. Terms such as 'cross-curricular links', 'inter-disciplinary enquiry', 'integrated curriculum', 'language across the curriculum', 'mathematics across the curriculum', 'life skills' and 'whole school policies' sound plausible but are often only tackled at an administrative level, concentrating purely on content overlap.

3. Although well intentioned, 'thematic' projects can suffer from the subject matter becoming trivial and contrived, especially as far as mathematics is concerned.

4. Both in inter-departmental meetings and in 'thematic' projects there is a strong danger that mathematics is seen and discussed only as a 'service subject', especially with regard to 'low attainers'.

5. Most of the problems encountered in working across the curriculum are due to, and exacerbated by, the enormous lack of awareness that exists in schools about what everyone else is doing, and about the nature of different subjects. This is especially true of mathematics where strange preconceptions are rife.

6. Whilst each subject area makes a unique contribution to the curriculum, all share a common concern for the development of pupils' knowledge, skills and attitudes.

**Recommendations**

1. Preconceptions about the nature and difficulty of mathematics must be tackled if any meaningful cross-curricular work involving the subject is to be developed.

2. If pupils of all abilities are both to (i) experience the richness of individual subjects and (ii) gain an overview of the subtle inter-relationships and interactions that exist among disciplines, it is essential to maintain *both* the links and the separation between subjects.

3. Cross-curricular cooperation must be developed at teacher level and be based on a strong, shared working commitment.

4. Senior management must play a supportive, facilitating role through, for example, flexible timetabling and staffing. Where initiatives are imposed by management on their staff without those teachers being involved and committed, such initiatives are unlikely to be sustained.

5. If sustained, meaningful cross-curricular links are to be effected, then teachers must be provided with mechanisms to work together on a long term basis. This has the same implications for support and provision, both in and out of school, that are outlined in Chapter 4 – 'Teacher Development' and Chapter 5 – 'Widespread, Sustained Curriculum Development'.

# EVALUATING AND ASSESSING MATHEMATICS

8

A teacher wrote:

"I am involved in instruction and assessment of teachers on a Mountain Leadership course. Instruction takes place over a number of weekends and assessment takes place in North Wales over the period of a week.

At the end of the week, the dialogue that has taken place continuously with each potential leader is brought to a conclusion. We talk about their leadership, organisation, navigation, security on steep ground etc. If at the end of the week assessor and assessed *disagree* about capabilities then the main aim of the assessment week is not achieved.

Fortunately this rarely happens. Usually teachers leave more confident in some areas and aware of their weaknesses, and

how much they should limit their projects. They do so secure in the knowledge that someone with some experience agrees with them.

Since the course is part of a national scheme, there are certain obligatory elements. One evening, after spending all day navigating round the mountains, the teachers have to complete a written exam on 'Navigation'. This irritates them, and seems irrelevant. Some consider it insulting. In no case has anyone 'failed' the exam having performed adequately on the mountain. In some cases the reverse has happened!

Perhaps there are some lessons for me to transfer to my mathematics classroom."

This chapter is concerned with reasons for assessment. It also explores conflicts and contradictions within our system and outlines responsibilities and criteria for evaluating and assessing children's mathematics.

## SECTION A  REASONS FOR ASSESSING

Before we can consider how best to assess and evaluate pupils' mathematics, it is vital to ask why we do it.

Here are some pupils' perceptions:

> maths exams and assessments help you to get used to examinations which is very helpful
>
> I think that we are assessed to check that we understand what we are being taught. It is to make sure we don't just listen and then forget about it.
>
> The assessment shows how far we are ahead of other pupils on the same subject
>
> It judjes pupils and teachers ability to learn and teach
>
> of proving showing yourself what you have learned and what other people's reaction is to it is

There are number of reasons why we wish to assess our pupils. Some assessment pressures originate from perceived external requirements while others are more pupil centred. Six of these reasons are indicated below:

### 1. Making comparisons.

'Pupils like to know where they are.'

Assessment is often about no more than comparisons. Pupils are compared with each other, with a set standard and with themselves. A teacher wrote of his concern:

> "Assessment often involves ranking. It sometimes occurs as the end result, but it should not be the sole aim. Assessment should be more about finding out what the child can do. Putting pupils in rank order does not do this."

### 2. Accountability.

'I'll give them a test to prove they can do it.'

In answering the question 'Why do we assess our pupils?', a teacher said:

> "To justify our teaching methods."

The education system has always been required to justify itself in terms of 'results'. Thus the publication of examination results in local newspapers is seen by some as a way of making public the efficiency of the school and its teachers. A head of department said:

> "Why should I change? My examination results are good."

The kind of justification that emphasises such results can lead to the achievements and needs of a significant proportion of children ('the bottom 40%') and their teachers being ignored or devalued.

### 3. Communication.

'How's my Tracy getting on then?'

Teachers have a responsibility to communicate to parents and employers about the achievements and difficulties of their pupils. The search for an effective way of fulfilling this need is one in which teachers have been involved for many years. We create 'communication vouchers', ie examination results, profiles, termly grades and reports, most of which, by their nature, vastly simplify the child's situation in the mathematics classroom, and can be misleading. These impoverished 'vouchers' are then used widely by employers and others for selection purposes.

### 4. Assessment as part of the learning process.

An advisory teacher wrote:

> "I do not see how one can separate the business of teaching from that of assessing, since they are both going on together for so much of the time in normal classroom practice.
>
> Decisions which we are continually making as we teach – what questions to ask, when to intervene, how to answer – are all based on our assessment of the individual pupil's mathematical development.
>
> Over a period of time, a picture is built up from a larger number of little brush strokes, many of which, as they were made in 'live' discussion or activity, are only visible to the teacher."

Evaluating and Assessing Mathematics    65

## 5. Diagnosis.

Diagnostic tests have been used for many years in order to ascertain sources of children's difficulties. However, at a national level these tests often provide little information that is useful to the teacher in improving action in the classroom. Internal school tests, though well intentioned, often provide a negative diagnosis and reinforce pupils' failures in a way that can be emotionally distressing.

Two pupils wrote:

> I felt ill and I didn't want to do it. I thought I would get a very low mark.
>
> before a test I feel nervous
> after a test I feel scared
> because I think that all
> my answers are wrong

## 6. Self-evaluation.

An advisory teacher wrote:

". . . pupils themselves may know about their own achievement but many will still say, quite wrongly in my opinion, that they are 'hopeless at maths' simply because they do not have a good facility with number or have acquired this notion from previous experience."

It is essential to consider the value of any assessment to the person who is being assessed. Many pupils leave school with an unrealistically low view of their mathematical abilities and potential. Often these views depend upon whether or not they liked their teacher, whether they are male or female, parents' and teachers' perceptions and expectations, or what particular book they were using. Simplistic assessment procedures may exacerbate this situation.

# SECTION B    INCOMPATIBILITIES

There exists a clear conflict between external and internal motives for assessment. Our system is riddled with incompatibilities, inconsistencies and contradictions:

Aim:    Encourage cooperative working. Discussion will facilitate mathematical development.

Action:    Group work in the classroom.

Assessment:    'Can you write it up separately in your own words please as we'll need to know what each of you did.'

Teachers wrote:

"The trouble is with the instrument we use for doing the assessing. The picture is often only a snapshot of one small part of a person."

"Why use a badly focused snapshot taken by a total stranger?"

Teachers set a Mode 3 paper.

The external moderator complained because a question was too hard.

The pupils coped admirably.

Aim:    Encourage practical and problem solving work in the classroom so as to enable pupils to gain experience of using skills flexibly in context.

Assessment:    'Measure and weigh this stick, and record your results.'

The books are taken in. Sharon has done six pages of work and her teacher takes a long time writing comments and questions in her book before grading it a B.

The books are returned. Sharon quickly flicks through her work and says 'I got a B'.

Do grades actually stop our pupils evaluating themselves and their work?

Employers have more applicants than they can cope with. Decisions still have to be made. When questioned they put great emphasis on qualities such as common sense, flexibility, ability to think and make decisions, and ability to work cooperatively in a team.

When advertised, the main requirement for the job is 'Grade C or above in Mathematics'.

What does a grade C tell you about a pupil?

Investigative work is important.

→ We cannot assess it by timed written examination.

↓ Pupils see no investigative work in the examination papers.

↙ Investigative work is not important.

Pupils like investigative work.

↘ It is incorporated into timed tests and examinations.

↓ Pupils are fearful and stressed by these examinations.

↘ Pupils do not like investigative work.

The examination system is fair. It allows people from all backgrounds to compete on equal terms. The best people will 'win'.

Fairness is sought by teachers, pupils and parents.

Mark schemes are scrupulously checked – half a mark for this, two marks for that.

Everyone must do their own unaided work.

No cheating.

Objectivity is provided by an outsider as examiner.

How fair is this to the pupil who consistently scores 3%?

Teachers, dissatisfied with percentages, grades and rankings, and seeing little communication value coming from 'average 43.22%, 28th out of 34', or even from 'effort B, achievement D', design a leaver's profile which they feel gives a better picture of their pupils' mathematical abilities.

Employers set an entrance test involving complex manipulations of fractions, decimals and imperial/metric conversions.

On a course, two groups of teachers were assessing the same pieces of pupil extended work.

One group graded them by 'gut feeling'. The other used criteria from various pieces of GCSE literature.

A teacher from the 'gut feeling' group apologised for not using the literature.

A teacher from the 'criteria group' said:

"Really, they were more honest than us. We spent most of our time manipulating the criteria grades to match up with our original gut feeling anyway."

A teacher wrote:

"The performer prefers to have his performance related to those of a roughly similar status. He does this in order to obtain feedback so that he can improve his status within that group, a major point of motivation."

Another teacher wrote:

"Children themselves may like to know where they stand in relation to others, but do the less able really need to know the true facts – don't they know already about their ability? Why rub it in?"

How motivating is rank order when you are always bottom?

**STATEMENT 33**
**If assessment is to be useful and not inhibitive to the pupil then any assessment structure or process must not be designed principally to meet the needs of any external agency. Effective communication to these external agencies about pupils' mathematical achievements and abilities can only be achieved and developed collaboratively.**

**RESPONSIBILITIES FOR ASSESSMENT**

A head of department wrote:

"A member of my department was off sick and my 'free' period that day coincided with a lesson when he would have been taking a second year class. I decided I would use the opportunity to find out some of their views on assessment. I asked them to write down what in their opinion would be the best way (or ways) for me to find out how 'good' they are at Mathematics.

On reading their replies later, I found the overwhelming majority suggested that:

(i)  I should ask their teacher.

(ii) I should teach them myself for a week or two."

Three of the pupils' responses are below:

The best possible way of telling how well we are doing is too ask us as we are the only ones besides our teacher that knows.
A test doesn't really tell you how we are getting on !!!

The best way. is to coming in to our class and ask us questions, to come round a talk to us. To help us then you would know what we do not know. Also to talk to our teacher.

I don't agree with tests. You are scared and rush your work. You work better with your friends. I think that a teacher should sit a in on a lesson, walking around and looking at peples works talking to the children and asking their teacher about their work.

It is often held that objectivity is paramount in any assessment, and yet it is self-evident that the people who know most about pupils' mathematical achievements are their teachers. An advisory teacher commented:

"Surely no external testing procedure can be without some of the undesirable side-effects associated with traditional examinations, and, for those who worry excessively about standardisation, it needs to be said loud and clear that the results they produced were far from being perfectly reliable; perhaps even more important is that they could only assess a very restricted range of mathematical processes and strategies.

I believe we must work to develop systems in which a large part of any 'grade' is a reflection of the very rich assessment picture built up in the course of teaching, and that the very essence of such a system must be the enhancement of teachers' sensitivity and confidence in their own assessment, and public recognition and trust of their judgement."

Mathematics teachers are expected to set regular tests. Hence there is a temptation to think that everything can be tested by a timed written paper. After sitting a one hour examination consisting of a single open ended problem a third year girl summed up the mismatch between the form of assessment and the problem given:

> I didn't like the exam. It was useless I don't think I learnt anything other than you need more than 1 hour to complete an investigation.

**STATEMENT 34**
**Teachers are best placed to take responsibility for effectively assessing their own pupils, and they need support in developing appropriate skills.**

Many teachers lack the confidence to take on this responsibility. Teachers are devalued by external bodies such as examination boards and universities who in general have had control of the examination system and its associated finance and research emphasis. This lack of control has led teachers to question their capabilities. We have found that when teachers have been actively involved in developing and modifying their own assessment procedures in departmental and inter-school groups, they begin to trust their own judgement, and realise their own expertise. One such teacher wrote:

"Examinations at any level should be organised by teachers since they are the people who know about the pupils. Obviously the needs of employers should be taken into account but teachers must have the conviction to fight for what they know is best for children.

Examinations, as with any form of assessment, are an integral part of the process of curriculum design, evaluation and development. To allow them to be organised from outside the teaching profession takes a major part of this possibility of change away from those most likely to be able to take advantage of it."

This direct involvement has also enabled teachers to articulate confidently their needs in terms of resources. A head of department wrote:

"To fulfil the requirements of GCSE we will have to change many of our practices, methods and attitudes. There is a need for staff development to implement the spirit of GCSE.

Effective change takes time and effort, and working in isolation would inhibit things. A regular meeting together will enable us to exchange ideas collected from visits to teacher centres, others' schools, courses etc."

If teachers are active participants in either the evolution or interpretation of the aims behind innovations, there is less likelihood that the initiatives will be looked upon as just another external requirement beyond the teachers' control, with the original aims being misrepresented in the classroom. It is easy to see, for example, how the provision of what are considered to be helpful assessment devices can harm the assessment process. The tasks of filling in checklists or seeking prescribed outcomes can take over and become aims in themselves, overriding the needs of the pupils and teachers concerned. Direct regular teacher involvement is even more essential as the assessment of oral, practical and extended work is more widely introduced. Although

GCSE offers broad opportunities for this kind of teacher involvement in the assessment process, it is not enough that these opportunities simply exist. (*See Chapter 3 – 'Aims and Actions'.*)

> **STATEMENT 35**
> **If children are to benefit from the intended changes in our asssessment, then communication must not reach them and their teachers at the end of a long chain. Direct, active involvement is essential at all levels.**

The false economies inherent in short cutting the development process are already having an effect as teachers under pressure are taking on attractive 'GCSE packages' that claim to provide easy solutions to their assessment problems. Even though it is certain that some money is needed for books, materials and equipment, in many cases these resources are requested because teachers have not had the time and opportunity available to examine their needs. The pressures imposed by commercial publishers help to fuel their anxiety. We have found that when teachers have been allowed time for development, they have been more able to use new and existing materials imaginatively and effectively, and have become more confident in their abilities to evaluate and assess their pupils' mathematics. As a result they are more able to use and interpret assessment models sensitively. Hence, the top priority for expenditure must be the provision of time for teachers to work collaboratively in ways that embody the features outlined in Chapter 4 – 'Teacher Development'.

In order to implement a continuous assessment model that has the pupils' interests as a priority, it is essential to create an atmosphere in the classroom where self-evaluation and dialogue are encouraged. Marking work is regarded as a teacher's duty and an important factor in maintaining standards of work. If, however, it is solely about ticks and crosses, or the aggregation of totals, or superficial comments such as 'Very good', or 'A good effort', or 'Merit', then it is difficult to see how it can help foster, in pupils, internal criteria for evaluating their mathematics. On the other hand, when marking is used to encourage a continuing dialogue, with pupils answering teachers' questions and comments, and teachers in turn responding, self-evaluation is nurtured, and self-awareness increased. Where assessment schemes are rigid in terms of allocating marks for prescribed outcomes (eg 4 for 'Generalisation', 6 for 'the Conclusion') they are likely to limit and channel pupils' mathematics as well as inhibit genuine dialogue and self-evaluation.

A working group of teachers, concerned that their assessment and evaluation of their pupils should assist in and be part of the learning process, developed the following criteria for use in their schools.

- Assessment procedures must not dictate what happens in the classroom.

- Any assessment scheme must acknowledge positive achievement.

- Assessment must be a continuing process involving dialogue between pupil/pupil, teacher/pupil and teacher/teacher.

- *All* teachers must be involved in the development of their departmental assessment procedures.

- Departmental assessment structures should allow an agreed measure of individual autonomy for teachers to assess their pupils in a way which does not compromise their relationships.

- Any assessment structure must be flexible enough to enable pupils to demonstrate their knowledge, understanding and actions in the form considered most appropriate by them and their teacher.

- Any decision made or action taken as a result of an assessment must involve the pupil.

- Assessment should not be seen as being solely in the hands of teachers. Pupils should be encouraged to evaluate and assess their own work.

- The fundamental aim of any assessment should be for the pupils to be able to feel confident about assessing and evaluating themselves.

These proposals have grown out of teachers' experiences in the classroom. If they are to become widespread and be sustained it is essential that the external system, including parents and employers, recognise and support them.

*Strategies for involving parents are explored in Chapter 9 – 'Parents'.*

## SUMMARY

### The situation

1. Teachers are best placed to take responsibility for effectively assessing their own pupils.

2. Assessment is often about no more than placing pupils in rank order. This reflects an ingrained belief in our society that people need to 'know where they are'.

3. Our present methods for communicating pupils' mathematical achievements to parents and employers generally do not provide useful or usable information.

4. Diagnostic tests often provide only a negative diagnosis and reinforce pupils' failures in a way that can be emotionally distressing.

5. Lack of control over assessment has led many teachers to question their capabilities.

6. The provision of what are considered to be helpful assessment devices can sometimes override the needs of pupils and teachers thus harming the assessment process.

7. There are attempts to short cut the developmental process. Teachers under pressure are taking on attractive packages that claim to provide easy solutions to their assessment problems. This is a false economy.

### Recommendations

1. In order to facilitate pupils' mathematical development, assessment must be an integral part of the learning process.

2. Helpful diagnostic exploration must be achieved through a continual dialogue which also identifies and acknowledges positive achievement.

3. It is essential to consider the value of any assesssment to the person who is being assessed. If the process does not allow for pupils to leave school thoroughly versed in self-evaluation, then the assessment process must be considered incomplete. Pupils must be actively encouraged to evaluate and assess their own work.

4. If assessment is to be useful and not inhibitive to pupils then assessment structures or processes must not dictate what is done in the classroom or be designed principally to meet the needs of external agencies.

5. Effective communication about pupils' mathematical achievements and abilities must be achieved and developed in collaboration with external agencies.

6. In order to support teachers in developing appropriate assessment skills the top priority for expenditure must be the provision of time for teachers to work collaboratively in ways that embody the features outlined in Chapter 4 – 'Teacher Development'.

7. If assessment is to be meaningful and support the curriculum then it is essential that the external system, including parents and employers, recognise and support the proposals outlined in this chapter.

# 9

# PARENTS

Who is our education for?

Who should make the demands?

Who knows best?

The teacher? The child? The parent . . .?

The following remarks were overhead at a mathematics parents' evening:

"My daughter spent hours on her homework doing long division. She was very upset so I tried to help. When I looked, she had got them right, but she was in tears. She didn't understand them."

"I'm not very good at maths and neither is my daughter."

"If my teacher hadn't beaten hell out of me and made me do it, I wouldn't be where I am today."

"I'm worried about the different ways teachers work. They are getting on well with a teacher and are doing well when suddenly they are moved on to the next teacher who has completely different ideas about maths, and the children suffer. They don't know where they are."

The whole area of parent/teacher relationships is riddled with misunderstandings.

| **What parents believe about teachers** | **What teachers believe about parents** |
| --- | --- |
| 'They aren't as good as they used to be.' | 'They don't really appreciate or understand what goes on in schools.' |
| 'They don't really understand my child.' | 'Parents won't like or support change.' |
| 'Teachers are too busy to be bothered with parents.' | 'The parents we want to see never come to parents' evenings.' |

Most teachers and parents will be able to provide other examples from their own experiences.

The relationship between teachers and parents is complex. Both groups have a strong commitment to the same children. Both teachers and parents have strong memories of their own schooling. Both groups are vulnerable and easily threatened. It is not surprising that such misunderstandings exist when useful and effective communication is so difficult to achieve. Whenever there is a lack of communication, suspicion and anxiety are likely to occur. Interestingly these tensions are still evident when teachers themselves are parents. This mathematics teacher writes about his concern when he thought his daughter might be about to be placed in a low set in the subject:

"My wife phoned a friend whose children were older and at the school. Yes, Mr. Johns took lower ability children in the second year when they were in it. Yes, there were eight groups – apparently by abilities – when they were in it. It could have changed . . .

Why did we not phone Mr. Johns? I don't know why there is this resistance to initiating such contacts, but it is there. Perhaps it is to do with the feeling that it will draw too much attention to my daughter, and that the teachers will not handle this sensitively.

I don't want to be labelled a 'fussy parent'. If this had been the primary school I would have gone in. Why is there a greater 'distance' between teachers and parents at secondary school level?"

The cumulative effect of the lack of parent/teacher dialogue and involvement can lead to very negative attitudes. Often parents feel that the only channel open to them is to write to the school. This distressing letter from a parent is an example in which a number of resentments are aired together:

"Owen has not done his homework as we cannot understand just what he has to do.

I would like to know what finding monkeys in trees has to do with maths, therefore I would be grateful if in future you could give him maths homework and not silly party games.

If this is the standard it is no wonder children are leaving school unable to read, write or do maths. Maybe before striking for more pay etc. you would do the job you're paid for."

Often teachers cite parents as a reason for not implementing curriculum change. Frequently they are concerned about parents' preconceptions as to what mathematics should be about. For example two teachers wrote:

"Parental anxiety in respect of the education of their children is very natural and they will resent any change from what they regard as the 'right' or 'accepted' way of doing maths."

"Parents like to see books with 'sums' they can understand and lots of ticks."

We have found, however, that when teachers are themselves more confident about why they are changing their approach in the classroom, parental involvement is welcomed. Teachers wrote:

"Remember parents care, are anxious, and will be your greatest ally if their children enjoy maths and don't feel it's a waste of time."

"Whatever we do it has to be a two way process where teachers have open minds too. We should learn from each other."

**STATEMENT 36**
**No sustained change can be effected unless parents are involved in, aware of, and support the developments taking place. Excluding parents is to deny a large part of the experience that pupils bring with them to school.**

Schools do make many efforts to communicate with parents, with varied amounts of success. For most parents and teachers, contact is made only at consultative evenings and therefore parents get little chance to appreciate the nature of the changes involved in mathematics teaching and learning. When specific mathematics evenings are held, they are often about no more than passing on information, consisting of lectures from heads of departments followed by questions from the more articulate and confident parents. We have found that more useful involvement is achieved through parents themselves taking part in mathematical activities, thereby experiencing the positive aspects of the subject. A teacher proposed:

"It is necessary to encourage parents to participate in the changed curriculum in order that they do not feel in the dark or threatened.

Meetings need to be occasions where parents can take part in activities. In short we need to involve parents to gain their support."

Where this kind of direct involvement has been encouraged, parents have become very positive in their support of developments in mathematics teaching of the kind outlined in Chapter 2 – 'Children Learning Mathematics'.

The following quotations are from parents who wrote of their feelings after attending a day in their children's school doing mathematics and talking with teachers. This day was the first of what has become a regular occurrence.

"I thoroughly enjoyed my day at school because I found the methods of learning much more interesting than when I was at school."

"There was more than one way of solving some of the problems. You had to use your initiative and put forward different ideas to come up with the right answers."

"I was pleasantly surprised to find that school mathematics involved a much more interesting and brain teasing set of problems to solve."

"I enjoyed the challenge of solving problems."

"The work was very different from my own school work of 20 years ago. I had to think for myself, instead of copying work from the blackboard."

"There was an air of good humour among the parents, who for the most part were total strangers to each other when we first arrived, but who I'm sure by the end of the day became very good friends."

"At the beginning of the morning I felt a slight reluctance to try anything, and thought that a child with little confidence would feel the same. However, as I progressed and got over the first hurdle, my confidence increased and I became very absorbed in the questions."

"I can now see how teaching methods will relate to the new exams, which will get pupils to think, rather than to learn parrot fashion."

There are many strategies for facilitating this kind of parental involvement. Some which teachers have used and found to be successful are indicated below:

- Inviting pupils to explain the work to parents.

  One parent commented that hearing his daughter go through what she had done enabled him to appreciate how much thinking and problem-solving had gone into the work.

- Sending work home to be done by the pupils with their parents.

  This not only allows parents to experience the type of work their children are doing but can also serve to open up communication.

  A teacher wrote:

"Justin had taken a problem home with him that he couldn't do in class. The next day he said, 'Miss, you know that puzzle we were doing yesterday? Well I gave it to my Mum to do and she took simply ages!'

It had obviously boosted Justin's confidence."

- Inviting parents to work alongside pupils on some mathematics.

- Inviting parents into school for the day.

  Two parents wrote after such a day:

  "I would definitely like to repeat the process, perhaps regularly."

  "I was stimulated and motivated to come again."

- Encouraging pupils to run mathematical sessions for the parents.

- Presenting parents with contrasting methods of teaching the same thing.

  On one evening parents were given a worksheet on long multiplication to complete. They were then invited to explore multiplication patterns on a table-square. In both cases there was a need to perform multiplication sums, and for many parents the richness of the table-square approach was highlighted.

- Asking parents who are already involved to:

  (a) run sessions;

  (b) get other parents involved.

- Encouraging local community centres such as libraries, leisure centres, town halls etc. to host exhibitions.

  Some teachers have found it beneficial to have pupils manning the displays, talking about their work and inviting involvement.

**STATEMENT 37**
**It is essential that any initiative designed to involve parents is not seen as a one-off activity. If effective and useful communication is to be achieved such involvement must be on a regular basis.**

Direct involvement of the kind outlined in this chapter is essential in gaining the support of employers as well as parents. It is only when this involvement is taking place that the full potential of community support can be realised. The potential is indeed great, when it is considered what facilities are available. The following ideas, some of which have been tried, are part of our agenda for action:

- Family mathematics workshops held in community centres.

- 'Ideal Home' type mathematics exhibitions consisting of workshops, including the use of computers and electronic devices, displays of equipment and chances to use them, discussion groups and videos with realistic strategies for follow-ups.

- Regular local radio and television 'mathematics spots'.

- Joint mathematics workshops with local artisans. Frequently people do not realise how much mathematics there is in their profession or craft, and how much mathematics they already know.

One parent said:

"My husband will be delighted to know that what he is doing is maths. He always thought he was bad at it."

Most of what we advocate here would not be considered unusual in other areas of the curriculum; for example local history, recreation and sport, science and technology. Failure to consider mathematics as worthy of such events is often because of the lack of awareness about the presence of mathematics in these activities, and also the lack of appreciation of the subject's intrinsic fascination. This appreciation can only come through the active involvement outlined earlier in this chapter.

The initiatives for the types of mathematics community project proposed here must not come solely from teachers. Parents, local employers and local councils all have a responsibility to help raise awareness through, for example, the discussion of the issues at local committees, as well as offering accommodation, skills, display facilities, publicity and manpower.

## SUMMARY

### The situation

1. Useful and effective communication is difficult to achieve because of the complex nature of the relationship between parents and teachers.

2. The whole area of parent/teacher relationships is riddled with misunderstandings because of a lack of communication.

3. The cumulative effect of the lack of parent/teacher dialogue and involvement can lead to very negative attitudes.

4. Often teachers cite parents as reasons for not implementing curriculum change. Frequently they are concerned about parents' preconceptions as to what mathematics should be about.

5. When teachers are themselves more confident about why they are changing their approach in the classroom, parental involvement is more likely to be welcomed.

6. No sustained change can be effected unless parents are involved in, aware of and support the developments taking place. Excluding parents is to deny a large part of the experience that pupils bring with them to school.

7. When specific mathematics evenings are held, they are often about no more than passing on information, consisting of lectures from heads of departments followed by questions from the more articulate and confident parents.

8. Where the kind of active involvement outlined in this chapter has been achieved, parents have become very positive in their support of developments in mathematics teaching of the kind outlined in Chapter 2 – 'Children Learning Mathematics'.

### Recommendations

1. More useful parental involvement must be achieved through parents taking part in mathematical activities themselves thereby experiencing the positive aspects of the subject.

2. It is essential that any initiative designed to involve parents is not seen as a one-off activity. If effective and useful communication is to be achieved, such involvement must be on a regular basis. Strategies for facilitating parental involvement are outlined in this chapter.

3. Direct involvement of the kind outlined in this chapter is essential in gaining the support of employers as well as parents.

4. In addition to school-focused activities, initiatives need to be made widespread throughout the community. Some strategies for this are outlined in this chapter.

5. The initiatives for the types of mathematics community project proposed in this chapter cannot come solely from teachers. Parents, local employers and local councils all have a responsibility to help raise awareness.

**10**

# EPILOGUE

In conversations and discussions we have found that certain misconceptions have arisen with regard to the Project and its work. Some examples are below:

**It has been said that:**

Our main aim is that pupils and teachers should enjoy their mathematics lessons more.

*See Chapter 2 – 'Children Learning Mathematics', pages 21–23*

**We are saying that:**

Our main aim is that pupils should attain a higher standard in the subject, and the strategies we advocate to achieve this certainly generate greater motivation, enjoyment and confidence. These positive attitudes to mathematics are a major factor in enabling pupils to achieve greater success and to apply their knowledge and skills to other areas of their life.

---

We think you can learn everything by 'investigations'.

*See Chapter 2 – 'Children Learning Mathematics', page 20*
*See Chapter 6 – 'Schemes', pages 48–49, 53*

'Investigations' must not be seen as new 'topics' to be covered on top of existing syllabus work. An enquiry approach – inviting pupils to question, challenge, discuss, interpret and explore – should pervade *all* mathematics learning. Conventional 'topics' such as percentages, trigonometry or algebra are rich areas for this kind of exploration.

---

We think children should never be helped or told what to do by their teacher.

*See Chapter 2 – 'Children Learning Mathematics', pages 14–20*

Teachers have a responsibility to act as catalysts in order to ensure that opportunities exist for children to take greater responsibility for their own learning. Pupils need to be encouraged to challenge their assumptions and develop their own strategies for dealing with mathematics. The teacher's role is essential here in helping pupils through stimulating, coordinating, focusing, challenging, supporting and facilitating.

---

| **It has been said that:** | **We are saying that:** |
|---|---|
| We think teachers need only administrative help from advisers and other in-service providers – that all teacher development needs is a room with a kettle where teachers can 'work together'. | In-service providers have a responsibility to act as catalysts in order to ensure that opportunities exist for teachers to take greater responsibility for their own development. Teachers need to be encouraged to challenge their assumptions and develop their own strategies for dealing with their own particular classrooms. The in-service provider's role is essential here in helping teachers through stimulating, coordinating, focusing, challenging, supporting and facilitating. |

*See Chapter 4 – 'Teacher Development'*

| | |
|---|---|
| The classroom approaches we advocate need 'special' teachers. | *All* teachers can become more confident and effective in the classroom. It is often the case that when teachers begin to work together and become more successful, they are seen and reclassified as 'special' teachers. |

*See Chapter 4 – 'Teacher Development'*

| | |
|---|---|
| Class size is not one of our concerns. | An improvement in the staff/pupil ratio is important. As teaching is such an isolated job, rather than a simple reduction in class size, it will be more beneficial in many cases to use the improved ratio to encourage collaborative teaching (eg two teachers working together with one larger class). |

*See Chapter 4 – 'Teacher Development', pages 34–35*
*See Chapter 7 – 'Working Across the Curriculum', pages 59–61*

| | |
|---|---|
| We expect teachers to give up a good deal of their free time. | Money and time for regular teacher release to work both in and out of school is essential for the kind of teacher development advocated by the Project. Creative timetabling can also allow development work with colleagues to take place in school time on a regular basis. |

*See Chapter 1 – 'Introduction', pages 5–6*
*See Chapter 4 – 'Teacher Development', pages 36–37*

| | |
|---|---|
| We think all development must be 'bottom up', beginning with teachers in the classroom, and that senior management have no part to play in the process. | Improvements and change can only be sustained if teachers in the classroom believe in and support the developments taking place. Impositions from above are therefore unlikely to work. Senior management has a positive, creative role to play. Their active involvement and organisational support are essential to sustain initiatives. |

*See Chapter 3 – 'Aims and Actions'*
*See Chapter 4 – 'Teacher Development', pages 32–34, 36–37*
*See Chapter 5 – 'Widespread, Sustained Curriculum Development', pages 42–44*
*See Chapter 7 – 'Working Across the Curriculum', pages 58–59*

| It has been said that: | We are saying that: |
|---|---|
| Our dissemination depends on a small group of apparently successful and enthusiastic individuals. | Dissemination must always be firmly rooted in the personal experiences of teachers in their classrooms. This is achieved through a constantly growing and developing network of personal contact and involvement – a cellular growth model of expansion. This is a long term, continuous process. |

*See Chapter 5 – 'Widespread, Sustained Curriculum Development'*

| | |
|---|---|
| We think publishing 'schemes' cannot bring about a widespread improvement in the quality of children's mathematics learning. | We think publishing 'schemes' cannot bring about a widespread improvement in the quality of children's mathematics learning. |

*See Chapter 5 – 'Widespread, Sustained Curriculum Development'*
*See Chapter 6 – 'Schemes'*

| | |
|---|---|
| We think published schemes and guidelines have no place in a mathematics department. | Where such schemes are used and recognised as short term vehicles for staff development they may be useful. However, they cannot short cut the longer term investment in teacher development that is necessary, and may actually inhibit the process. |

*See Chapter 6 – 'Schemes', pages 48–54*

| | |
|---|---|
| We think assessment always inhibits the learning process. | Sensitive assessment schemes must be an integral part of the work going on in the classroom, and hence support the mathematics curriculum. Therefore pupils should be actively involved in their own assessment, and fully understand the process. |

*See Chapter 8 – 'Evaluating and Assessing Mathematics'*

| | |
|---|---|
| The changes in mathematics teaching we advocate will not be supported by parents. | When parents are directly involved in, and aware of, the developments taking place in the classroom they actively support the work their children are doing in mathematics. |

*See Chapter 9 – 'Parents'*

## FUTURE WORK

The Project's work is ongoing. The network of teachers in the six Local Education Authorities continues to grow and will continue to need support and provision of the kind indicated throughout this report.

A new DES-funded Project, RAMP (Raising Achievement in Mathematics Project 1986–9), will operate in a similar way to this Project. RAMP initially covers 34 Local Education Authorities including the six already involved in the south. Our methodology requires that the new Project will work at the issues and needs of the teachers in their classrooms. The areas and schools have been chosen so that specific attention will be drawn to certain wider issues including parental and community involvement, cross-curricular work, cultural and ethnic minority issues, sixth form implications and effects on higher education courses. Ongoing work with the primary and special needs sectors will be reinforced.

An area of particular concern for the future is sixth form mathematics. This issue has emerged from the Project as one needing further attention. This is highlighted by the following GCSE examiners' comments on a Mode 3 GCSE submission:

"We wish to congratulate the two schools heartily on the particular quality of this submission, which augurs well for the future of mathematics teaching and learning in this country. . . . we anticipate that this submission will lead to mathematics teaching and learning of the highest calibre, giving an early fulfilment of what was envisaged in the National Criteria . . . but feel that your candidates may have at least initial difficulties in coping with current A level courses of a more traditional nature."

However, these teachers, and others associated with the Project who have sixth form classes, have already been working in the same way with them as with their other pupils, and with great success. This overall change in their teaching approach has also resulted in increased numbers of pupils opting for mathematics courses leading to 'A' level.

Even though a more enquiry-based teaching approach has been successful with these traditional 'A' level courses, their present content and emphasis leave much to be desired. Often the pressures of covering content in order to ensure examination success lead to a moral dilemma for teachers in that they feel obliged to teach in ways that they know will restrict their students' mathematical diet. Added to this problem are the new sixth form students whose interests and creative mathematical ideas must now be catered for, and the need to acknowledge and incorporate the exploratory potential of computers at this level. For example, technology provided by computers now enables students to experiment with a whole range of graphs of relations and their behaviour in the same time as they would have taken to plot the graph of a single ellipse from its standard equation. The service role of new technology to applied subjects such as engineering must also seriously question what it is that mathematics courses at sixth form need to provide.

Although the progression of enquiry-based work into the sixth form has been more of a natural one for those teachers with sixth forms attached to their schools, problems can be exacerbated where institutions such as sixth form colleges have not been involved in developments further down the age range. If widespread improvements in the quality of mathematics teaching and learning are to be brought about for the 16+ age range, then teachers from these institutions must also be allowed time for the kind of professional development advocated throughout this report. One teacher in a sixth form college highlighted the problem:

". . . the main aim of the department has been expressed as 'to achieve maximum examination success'. Even for those more aware of recent developments the awareness and involvement is very superficial as it hasn't touched their classrooms. While the A level ethos and content doesn't change, all development work for GCSE, 17+, CPVE etc. is seen as a necessary nuisance to be suffered for a minority of students."

There exist many new initiatives designed to broaden the curriculum for students in this age group (CPVE, 'AS' levels, etc.). Where senior management and subject specialists resist such changes in the belief that present syllabuses at 'O' and 'A' level are 'what the students need' and 'what their parents want', developments in mathematics of the kind supported by the Project's work will be difficult to implement and sustain.

Universities have considerable influence in determining perceptions and practice in mathematics teaching. This has the potential either to facilitate or inhibit change. Where universities are unaware of developments in pre-university mathematics teaching and learning, including the use of computers in mathematics, and where the courses they offer do not provide students with opportunities for engaging in creative and exploratory work, their influence will continue to be inhibitive. Many lecturers cite reasons similar to those expressed by teachers for not changing their teaching approaches – pressure of time, syllabus content etc. These issues need to be addressed. For future developments to have national significance, universities and other higher education institutions cannot be excluded from the continuous process of curriculum development.

# PROJECT REVIEW

The purpose of this Review is to set out briefly the background, initial aims, emphasis and outcomes of LAMP. In addition it outlines the nature and areas of future work and contains a selection of the Project's recommendations. (For the full recommendations see the Summary of each chapter.)

LAMP was a DES/LEA-funded post-Cockcroft curriculum development project. The following extract is taken from the Project's original detailed proposal to the DES in 1983:

"The West Sussex Institute Mathematics Centre has served as a regional focus in this area of work over a number of years by providing full and part time courses and conferences, and working with local curriculum development groups. This work has grown out of experience gained over the past ten years in mounting National and Regional DES courses for teachers of slow learners in mathematics. These courses are being extended. The Centre has well established links with the advisory staff and teachers in the authorities proposing to participate in this project. The project would provide an excellent opportunity for building upon a vast amount of experience, expertise and material already developed within the region. The proposed Director, Mr. A. Ahmed, was a member of the Cockcroft Committee and took part in the discussion on the secondary curriculum which involved reviewing the relevant research undertaken in this field."

The Project centred on 12 'teacher–researchers'. These classroom teachers were released by their local authorities for one day a week for the period of the Project to work collaboratively both at the Mathematics Centre and in schools. The six authorities involved (Dorset, East Sussex, Hampshire, Isle of Wight, Surrey and West Sussex) were enthusiastic to develop this initiative as a powerful means of implementing the ideas and proposals set out in the Cockcroft Report.

The original agreed Project aims were to:

1. encourage teachers to change their attitudes to the ways in which low attainers learn mathematics;

2. help teachers to interpret the Cockcroft Committee's 'foundation list' (para 458) in the spirit of paragraphs 455 to 457 and 460 to 466. That is, to suggest activities which should involve low attaining pupils in a wider range of mathematics than the usual restrictive diet of 'basics';

3. provide teachers with ideas and strategies which should enable pupils to change their perceptions of mathematics, encouraging them not to view the subject just as a body of knowledge to be 'passed on' fact by fact;

4. suggest ways in which teachers can continually gain insight into pupils' mathematics, without having to rely on formal tests;

5. suggest ways in which pupils can arrive at conventional methods and terminology through their participation in problem solving activities and investigatory mathematics;

6. develop ways of working which should enable pupils to see links between mathematics and other subject areas;

7. suggest ways of working which should help teachers to develop pupils' confidence and independence in handling mathematics;

8. suggest approaches which should help teachers cope with different rates of learning amongst low attainers.

Once work began it became clear to all those involved that low attainment was not a problem only for pupils in the 'bottom 40%' attainment range. They found the changes they were making in their teaching approaches were encouraging *all* their pupils to become more involved in their mathematics and to surpass traditional expectations at every level. The problem became one of under-achievement across the age and ability range.

If improved mathematics teaching and learning was to be widespread, then any action taken had to be seen to be within the complex situation of the classroom. Hence it was necessary for the teacher–researchers to sustain contact with all the day-to-day problems of school life such as difficult pupils and conditions, report writing, examinations and marking. To step back in the interests of 'objectivity' and to ignore these awkward realities of classroom life would have invalidated both the procedure and the outcomes of the Project's work.

The power of convictions in shaping behaviour is strong. If teachers do not believe that their pupils are capable of thinking for themselves then they are unlikely to give them the opportunities to do so. Similarly, if teachers themselves have a restricted view of the subject then their pupils' diet in mathematics lessons will be inadequate. This has been found to be a problem as much with well qualified mathematicians as with non-specialists. Hence a fundamental prerequisite of all the Project's curriculum development work has been to allow mathematics teachers time to question and challenge the implications of their beliefs. The Project's experience shows that without this, attempts to provide schemes, reports or guidelines on the teaching of mathematics are very likely to be misinterpreted or ignored, and at best their effects will be short lived.

The effectiveness of the Project's work depends upon its dissemination strategies. A cellular growth model of expansion ensures that all dissemination is through active personal involvement. Hence the curriculum development and research remain firmly rooted in the personal experiences of teachers in their classrooms. The success of this can be seen by the fact that the Project network is no longer centred around the 12 teacher–researchers. It is continually growing and developing as new working groups form and involve more teachers. To date some 2000 teachers in the region are involved in developing strategies for improving their pupils' mathematical attainment, confidence and interest.

The following illustrations demonstrate the quality of the developments brought about by those involved in the Project network.

1. *Pupils are achieving greater success in the subject.* This is true of pupils across the age and ability range both in terms of traditional examination success and in terms of their enjoyment, motivation, confidence and interest in mathematics. Their perceptions of the subject have broadened enabling them to apply their knowledge and skills to other areas of their life. *See Chapter 2 – 'Children Learning Mathematics' and Chapter 8 – 'Evaluating and Assessing Mathematics'.*

2. *The number of pupils choosing to take mathematics at 'A' level has increased. See Chapter 2 – 'Children Learning Mathematics'.*

3. *Teachers are finding greater satisfaction in their classrooms.* They see their children using and discussing mathematics in ways they do not expect, and their own interest in the subject has been reawakened and broadened. *See Chapter 4 – 'Teacher Development'.*

4. *The work has not been limited to individual teachers' classrooms.* Departments are working together and in many cases senior management have facilitated developments through organisational initiatives and support. *See Chapter 3 – 'Aims and Actions' and Chapter 4 – 'Teacher Development'.*

5. *Teachers' views of their own professional responsibilities have widened.* They are, for example, more willing to take on issues concerning assessment initiatives, new technology and resourcing. Membership of the professional mathematical associations has increased in the region, with many teachers now actively contributing to the journals and other publications for the first time in their careers. *See Chapter 3 – 'Aims and Actions' and Chapter 4 – 'Teacher Development'.*

6. *Teachers have become more discerning with regard to in-service provision, published material and other resources.* For example, they are not as willing to take on pre-packaged mathematics schemes when they see that the schemes do not encourage their pupils to develop mathematically through questioning, challenging, discussing, interpreting and exploring. Reference and practical materials, everyday articles and pupils' own interests are being used imaginatively in the classroom. Teachers are also more aware of the broad opportunities that exist with regard to mathematics learning within initiatives such as GCSE, TVEI etc. They are not as willing to participate in in-service courses that attempt to deal with issues on a superficial, detached level that they see as merely academic rather than genuinely professional. *See Chapter 4 – 'Teacher Development', Chapter 5 – 'Widespread, Sustained Curriculum Development' and Chapter 6 – 'Schemes'.*

7. *The enormous value of collaborative work between Local Education Authorities has been demonstrated by the Project.* The advisers had a common aim to involve more of their teachers and schools in the kind of professional development indicated throughout the report. Their cooperation, support and joint initiatives have been a major factor in the Project's success. *See Chapter 5 – 'Widespread, Sustained Curriculum Development'.*

8. *Support and working groups have been set up by teachers throughout the region.* They serve two vital purposes in ensuring that: (a) the teachers involved no longer feel isolated in their classrooms or schools and they learn from each others' experiences and (b) their self-appraisal skills are developed through classroom experimentation, reflection and discussion. The groups provide an important follow up to courses run in the region and through them the work of the teachers involved has directly influenced the emphasis of subsequent courses and curriculum developments within the Project authorities. The fact that the groups, once initiated, have been largely self-sustaining, flourished and have continued to grow throughout the period of the Project (1983–6) illustrates the importance attached to them by teachers. *See Chapter 5 – 'Widespread, Sustained Curriculum Development'.*

9. *The Project has had great influence on mathematics in-service provision for GCSE.* Teachers involved in the Project network have been widely used to initiate developments concerning extended coursework, oral and practical work, changing the climate in the classroom and more general assessment issues. Interactive in-service material, produced by a group of teachers involved in the network, is being widely used in schools across the country and abroad, on in-service courses, and is recommended by the Secondary Examinations Council. *See Chapter 5 – 'Widespread, Sustained Curriculum Development' and Chapter 8 – 'Evaluating and Assessing Mathematics'.*

10. *The Project has begun to have far reaching effects across the curriculum.* Cooperative teaching between subjects has been taking place and has resulted in greater understanding of common learning and teaching problems and aims. *See Chapter 7 – 'Working Across the Curriculum'.*

11. *Teachers have found that actively involving parents in the developments taking place has led to increased support.* This has greatly benefited the pupils. *See Chapter 9 – 'Parents'.*

12. *The Project has enabled teachers within the network to devise and contribute to a wide range of booklets containing ideas, strategies and case studies.* Although the production of material is in no way central to the Project's work, these resources are proving increasingly popular because of their relevance to classroom life and their interactive in-service potential. The work includes a substantial amount dealing with the imaginative and exploratory use of computers in mathematics, as well as some more extensive classroom studies. *See Chapter 6 – 'Schemes'.*

13. *The Project has been invited to make major contributions to conferences held in Britain and abroad.* Some involvements have been with the International Congress of Mathematics Education 5 in Adelaide, the Mathematical Association, the

National Association for Remedial Education, the Association of Teachers of Mathematics, and CIEAEM '86 (International Commission for the Study and Improvement of Mathematics Teaching) at Southampton. A UNESCO publication containing a chapter referring to the Project's work is available.

14. *The Project is playing an increasing consultancy role.* Advisers and advisory teachers from various authorities and lecturers and moderators from the Mathematical Association's Low Attainers Diploma Board are among others who have become involved with the Project network in this capacity. When approached by publishers, the Project has managed to influence policy decisions through engaging them in working at issues with teachers. This has encouraged them to consider the production of more flexible and usable resources. In conjunction with organisations such as the British Council and the Service Children's Education Authority (SCEA) similar consultancy has been provided abroad.

## FUTURE WORK

The Project's work is ongoing. The network of teachers in the six Local Education Authorities continues to grow and will continue to need support and provision of the kind indicated throughout the report.

A new DES-funded Project, RAMP (Raising Achievement in Mathematics Project 1986–9), will operate in a similar way to this Project. RAMP initially covers 34 Local Education Authorities including the six already involved in the south. The nature of the Project's work requires that RAMP will work at the issues and needs of the teachers in their classrooms. Ongoing work with the primary and special needs sectors will be reinforced. The areas and schools have been chosen so that more specific attention will be drawn to certain wider issues, including parental and community involvement, cross-curricular work, cultural and ethnic minority issues, sixth form implications and effects on higher education courses. *Further details can be found in Chapter 10 – 'Epilogue'.*

## RECOMMENDATIONS

**The report contains recommendations for action at the end of every chapter. They are relevant to all those involved with, and concerned about, school mathematics.**

At present the system itself is under-achieving. If we want to raise the level of educational provision in mathematics we must develop the professionalism of teachers, their confidence and their expertise, as ultimately they are the only people who can directly effect improvements in the quality of children's learning experiences. Through teachers' development, pupils' attainment and competence will be raised, enabling them to meet the needs of a modern society. With its emphasis on professional development, and its dissemination based on personal contact and cellular growth, the Project has demonstrated how this can be achieved.

The implications of the Project's experience is that financial and organisational provision must necessarily be flexible. Funding should enable the replication of the Project in other areas in order that curriculum development and classroom based research can become an integral part of a teacher's working life, with all the implications that this has for the substantial provision of time. However, to provide time without paying adequate attention to the quality of experience gained by teachers is of no value.

**With this quality of experience in mind the Project has identified certain ingredients which must be part of any sustained curriculum and professional development initiative in mathematics.**

1.  *Classroom teachers must be actively involved in their own in-service provision in order to develop their confidence, motivation, autonomy and professionalism in providing for their pupils' needs and in terms of their own mathematics. This must be a long term continuous process. Short cuts are a false economy.*

2.  *Sufficient time must be allowed on a* regular *basis within their working week for teachers to pool their classroom expertise, develop their own strategies, challenge their assumptions, reflect on classroom experiences and work collaboratively with colleagues.*

3.  *In-service providers must act as 'catalysts' in order to ensure that this regular professional development is stimulated and facilitated.*

4.  *Agencies such as initial training institutions with experience of facilitating in-service work of the kind described in 1, 2 and 3 above must be utilised to the full for the professional development of teachers. This should be both in terms of their human and their material resources.*

5.  *Releasing teachers for this kind of professional development must be achieved through extra staffing and through imaginative timetabling. When release is achieved through extra staffing these teachers must not be employed on an occasional ad hoc basis but must be incorporated in the normal staffing of a school so that continuity can be provided for the pupils.*

6.  *For developments to become widespread, dissemination must depend upon a cellular growth of working groups rather than on a written product.*

7.  *Where senior management, advisory staff, initial trainers, in-service providers, examining groups, parents etc. are involved, they must be seen as partners in the development. Within their own role or function they must be active participants.*

**From the Project's experience the above ingredients are as relevant to initiatives in other areas of the curriculum as they are to developments in mathematics.**

# ACKNOWLEDGEMENTS

The strength of the Project is in the large number of people who participate in it. These include all those teachers on present and past diploma courses based at WSIHE and those in support and other working groups throughout the six Project Local Education Authorities. It also includes those pupils, parents, employers and others who are involved with the Project's work. It would be impossible to list all these people separately, or describe their particular involvement. We wish, however, to acknowledge specifically the contributors listed below for their support.

- The following headteachers of the original Project schools and their staffs:

| | |
|---|---|
| Mr. T. A. Jackson | The Grange School, Dorset |
| Mr. L. W. Matthews (until Dec. 1984) and Mr. A. J. Murphy (from Jan. 1985) | St. Edwards R.C. School, Dorset |
| Mr. K. L. Saxby | Tideway School, East Sussex |
| Mr. J. Dalton | St. Vincent School, Hampshire |
| Dr. A. Leech | Bohunt School, Hampshire |
| Mr. M. J. Pipes | City of Portsmouth Boys' School, Hampshire |
| Mr. C. Burland (until March 1985) and Mr. I. Harwood (from April 1985) | Kitbridge Middle School, Isle of Wight |
| Mr. P. Connor | Ryde High School, Isle of Wight |
| Mr. D. P. Hannon (until July 1985) | Wayneflete School, Surrey |
| Mr. P. A. F. Newton (from Sept. 1985) | Trinity School, Surrey |
| Mr. M. D. Palmer | De Burgh School, Surrey |
| Mr. B. J. Groom (until Dec. 1984) and Mr. S. Lee (from Jan. 1985) | Downsbrook County Middle School, West Sussex |
| Mr. P. G. Stewart | St. Andrew's C.E. Boys' High School, West Sussex. |

- The members of the Steering Committee (Chairman: Professor Brian Griffiths) for their time and commitment, including visits to schools and to WSIHE to work with the teacher–researchers. The contributions of the Steering Committee secretaries, Alan Clarke and Stephen Dance, were invaluable.

- The advisers of the six Local Education Authorities for demonstrating the value of collaborative work between authorities.

- The director of WSIHE, Mr. J. F. Wyatt, and his senior and administrative staff for demonstrating how the human and material resources of an initial training institution can be utilised to the full for the professional development of teachers.

- The clerical staff of the Mathematics Centre at WSIHE, in particular the Project Secretary Jean Dann, for the essential coordinating, administrating and organising work necessary to the continual extension of the Project network.

- The other two post-Cockcroft studies, namely SSCC (SMP, Suffolk, Chelsea College, COSSEC (Cambridge, Oxford and Southern Secondary Examinations Council) Graduated Assessment in Mathematics), and NFER's Graduated Tests in Mathematics for Lower-Attaining Pupils, for our joint meetings and mutual questioning and support.

- The Mathematical Association, especially through the work of the Low Attainers Diploma Board, and the Association of Teachers of Mathematics for continued stimulation and challenge through their publications, to which Project teachers are able to contribute, their resource material and through individual contacts.

- Those who visit WSIHE to conduct seminars and workshops with the teacher–researchers. Their more distant, critical view of our work and their presentations of their own research provide essential challenges and ensure a continual dialogue with other initiatives and developments.

- Pam Bartlett, a teacher–fellow seconded from Birmingham LEA, for her sustained work alongside the teacher–researchers both in schools and at WSIHE in order to examine and identify the aspects of the Project that are transferable to other authorities.

- John Walpole, General Manager of the Chatsworth Hotel, Worthing, whose personal interest and insight as a local employer are invaluable. His position in the local business community and as a school governor enables him to involve a wide range of individuals and groups in the Project's work.

- Dr. Ray Peacock, Research Coordinator, Philips UK Ltd., whose stimulating and perceptive observations on the parallels between industry and education greatly encourage the Project's work. In his position as an international industrial researcher he has demonstrated enthusiastically that many of the Project's concerns are not limited to the education sector, but have far wider implications.

- Roy Potter, Director of Education, West Sussex County Council (until March 1985). Not only did his perspective as a modern linguist greatly increase awareness of the cross-curricular potential of the Project's work, but his advice, foresight and energetic support are instrumental in highlighting the national significance of the work being done in the six authorities.

- Henry Macintosh, Secretary of the Southern Regional Examinations Board, and the Board itself for supporting extensive development in conjunction with the Project. Henry Macintosh's wide ranging knowledge, experience and interests have enabled the Project to keep up to date with national and international developments in assessment and curriculum initiatives in all areas and across the age range.

With respect to the report itself we are particularly grateful to those listed below.

- The large number of individuals and groups for their time and commitment in responding to draft chapters of the report either through using them as in-service resources or through commenting on their substance. The feedback gained was an integral part of the production of the report.

- John Rickwood, Technical Director of Gower Consultants Ltd., for his contributions in terms of design work and cartoons. The fact that from his business perspective he is able to support the outcomes and identify with the concerns of the Project's work in this way has been of great value. The use of the company's computer facilities was essential to the physical production of the report.

- Frankie Sulke and John Mitchell for the time invested by them in shaping and structuring the report from all the collated evidence.

*Afzal Ahmed*

Afzal Ahmed, Project Director

# BIBLIOGRAPHY

The bibliography is divided into three sections:

A.  Curriculum development projects;

B.  Books and periodicals;

C.  Supporting publications.

**SECTION A**  CURRICULUM DEVELOPMENT PROJECTS

The following projects were examined in depth by LAMP because of shared aims and concerns and their influence on curriculum development. Much of the evidence was collated in the form of taped interviews, articles and personal writings by those involved.

Schools Council Project in Secondary School Mathematics – Mathematics for the Majority 1967–70

Schools Council Mathematics for the Majority Continuation Project 1971–74

Schools Mathematics Project 1961–

Midlands Mathematics Experiment 1962–

Schools Council Project on Statistical Education 1975–80

Schools Council Humanities Curriculum Project 1967–70

Success and Failure and Recent Innovation – Safari 1973–77

Progress in Learning Science Project – Match and Mismatch 1973–77

**SECTION B**  BOOKS AND PERIODICALS

A wide range of relevant books and periodicals have been listed in:

(1)  A review of research in mathematical education: Part A, Research on learning and teaching, Bell A.W., Costello J. and Kuchemann D., NFER-Nelson (1983)

and

(2)  Booklists – For the teaching of mathematics in schools, the Mathematical Association (1984).

We have identified a shorter list of books which have particularly influenced the Project team.

| ABERCROMBIE M.L.J. (1969) | The anatomy of judgement | Pelican |
| APU (1980–  ) | Mathematical development: secondary and primary reports | HMSO |
| ATM (1969) | Notes on mathematics in primary schools | Cambridge University Press |

| | | |
|---|---|---|
| ATM (1977) | Notes on mathematics for children | Cambridge University Press |
| ATM (1970) | Mathematical reflections | Cambridge University Press |
| ATM (1980) | Language and mathematics | ATM (Association of Teachers of Mathematics) |
| ATM (1966) | The development of mathematical activity in children | ATM |
| BATESON G. (1973) | Steps to an ecology of mind | Paladin |
| BEER S. (1975) | Platform for change | Wiley |
| BELL A.W., COSTELLO J. and KUCHEMANN D. (1983) | A review of research in mathematical education: Part A, Research on learning and teaching mathematics | NFER-Nelson |
| BISHOP A.J., NICKSON MARILYN (1983) | A review of research in mathematical education: Part B, Research on the social context of mathematics education | NFER-Nelson |
| BLANCHARD J. (1986) | Out in the open | Cambridge University Press |
| BOARD OF EDUCATION (1912) | The teaching of mathematics in the United Kingdom, Parts I and II | HMSO |
| BROOKES W.M. and UNDERWOOD V.L. (1970) | Development in mathematical education | School of Education, Southampton, ATM |
| BURGESS R.G. (1985) | Issues in educational research qualitative methods | Falmer Press |
| CARR W. and KEMMIS S. (1986) | Becoming critical | Falmer Press |
| COCKCROFT W.H. (Chairman) (1982) | Mathematics counts: report of the Committee of Enquiry | HMSO |
| COLLINGWOOD R.G. (1970) | An autobiography | Oxford University Press |
| DAVIS P.J. and HERSH R. (1981) | The mathematical experience | Pelican |
| DES (1979) | Aspects of secondary education | HMSO |
| DES (1984) | Slow learning and less successful pupils in secondary schools | DES |
| DES (1985) | Mathematics from 5 to 16: curriculum matters 3 | HMSO |
| DES (1985) | Curriculum from 5 to 16 | HMSO |
| DES (1985) | Technology and school science | HMSO |
| DES (1980) | A view of the curriculum | HMSO |
| DES (1985) | Better schools | DES |
| DICKSON L., BROWN M. and GIBSON O. (1984) | Children learning mathematics | Holt, Rinehart and Winston |
| DONALDSON M. (1978) | Children's minds | Fontana (London) |
| FITZGERALD A. (1985) | New technology and mathematics in employment | DES |
| FLETCHER T.J. (HMI) (1983) | Microcomputers and mathematics in schools | DES |
| FREUDENTHAL H. (1978) | Weeding and sowing | D. Reidel |

| | | |
|---|---|---|
| GATTEGNO C. (1970) | What we owe children | Routledge and Kegan Paul |
| GATTEGNO C. (1963) | For the teaching of mathematics Vol. 1. | Educational Explorers Ltd. |
| HARGREAVES D.H. (1972) | Interpersonal relations and education | Routledge and Kegan Paul |
| HARGREAVES D.H. (Chairman) (1984) | Improving secondary schools | Swindon Press Ltd. |
| HART K. (Ed.) (1981) | Children's understanding of mathematics: 11–16 | Murray |
| HEIDEGGER M. (1978) | Basic writings | Routledge and Kegan Paul |
| HMI (1982) | Mathematics in the sixth form | HMSO |
| HMI (1976) | Mathematics, science and modern language – an appraisal | DES |
| HOLT J. (1969) | How children fail | Pelican |
| HOWSON A.G. (1983) | A review of research in mathematical education: Part C, Curriculum development and curriculum research | NFER-Nelson |
| KLINE M. (1953) | Mathematics in Western culture | Oxford University Press |
| KRUTETSKII V.A. (1976) | The psychology of mathematical abilities in school children | University of Chicago Press |
| LAKATOS I. (1976) | Proofs and refutations: the logic of mathematical discovery | Cambridge University Press |
| MACNAB D.S. and CUMMINE J.A. (1986) | Teaching mathematics 11–16 | Basil Blackwell |
| MINISTRY OF EDUCATION (1958) | Teaching mathematics in secondary schools, Pamphlet no. 36 | HMSO |
| MORGAN J. (1977) | Affective consequences for the learning and teaching of mathematics of an individual learning programme | University of Stirling |
| OLDKNOW A. and SMITH D. (1983) | Learning mathematics with micros | Ellis Horwood Ltd. |
| OLDKNOW A. (1985) | Graphics with microcomputers | Nelson |
| PAPERT S. (1980) | Mindstorms: children, computers and powerful ideas | Basic Books Inc. |
| POLANYI M. (1962) | Personal knowledge | Routledge and Kegan Paul |
| POPPER K.R. (1978) | Conjectures and refutations | Routledge and Kegan Paul |
| ROGERS C. (1983) | Freedom to learn for the 80's | Charles Merrill |
| ROWNTREE D. (1977) | Assessing students: how shall we know them? | Harper and Row |
| RUTTER M. et al (1979) | Fifteen thousand hours: secondary schools and their effects on children | Open Books |
| SCHOOLS COUNCIL (1977) | Match and mismatch | Oliver and Boyd |
| SCHOOLS COUNCIL (1977) | Mixed ability teaching in mathematics | Evans/Methuen Educational |
| SEWELL B. (1982) | The use of mathematics by adults in daily life | Advisory Council for Adult and Continuing Education |
| STENHOUSE L. (1975) | An introduction to curriculum research and development | Heinemann |

| TAHTA D.G. (Ed) (1972) | A Boolean anthology. Selected writings of Mary Boole | ATM |
| WADDINGTON C.H. (1977) | Tools for thought | Paladin |
| WERTHEIMER M. (1961) | Productive thinking | Tavistock |
| WHITEHEAD A.N. (1932) | The aims of education | Williams and Norgate |
| WITTGENSTEIN L. (1976) | Philosophical investigations | Basil Blackwell |
| WITTGENSTEIN L. (1977) | On certainty | Basil Blackwell |
| YATES J. (1978) | Four mathematical classrooms | University of Southampton |

The following select periodicals also contain many important and relevant articles:

| Educational Studies in Mathematics | D. Reidel Publishing Company |
| For the Learning of Mathematics | FLM Publishing Association |
| Mathematics in School | Longman Group Ltd. on behalf of the Mathematical Association |
| Mathematics Teaching | ATM |
| Micromaths | ATM and Basil Blackwell |
| Struggle | ILEA and the Mathematical Association |
| Support for Learning – successor to Remedial Education | Journal of NARE |

<table>
<tr><td style="background:black;color:white">SECTION C</td><td></td></tr>
</table>

## SECTION C    SUPPORTING PUBLICATIONS

The following publications are directly associated with the Project. They include publications arising from the work of primary teachers involved with the Project. They take the form of booklets, working papers and in-service resources.

| AHMED A.G. | Implications of the Cockcroft report, in Mathematics for all, Science and Technology Education No. 20 | UNESCO (also published separately by WSIHE as 'Foundations of Mathematics for all') |
| AHMED A.G., BIDDLE A., SAVAGE C., SMITH T. and VOWLES L. | Mathematics for low attainers | WSIHE/West Sussex County Council |
| AHMED A.G., BUFTON N. (CO-DIRECTORS) | Teachers evaluating and assessing mathematics (TEAM) | Southern Region Examination Board/ WSIHE |
| BIRD M. | Beginning investigations | WSIHE |
| BIRD M. | Generating mathematical activity in the classroom | Mathematical Association |
| BIRD M. | Mathematics with 7 and 8 year olds, 8 and 9 year olds, 9 and 10 year olds and 10 and 11 year olds | Mathematical Association (Available as separate booklets) |
| BUFTON N. and SMITH D. | CHIMPS – Computer help in mathematics problem solving | WSIHE |

| | | |
|---|---|---|
| EVANS K. | Needs in the mathematics classroom – a study of fourth year low attaining pupils | WSIHE |
| LOW ATTAINERS MATHEMATICS PROJECT (LAMP) | Advisory teachers' discussion document | WSIHE |
| LAMP | Changes | WSIHE |
| LAMP | What is mathematics all about? | WSIHE |
| LAMP | Schemes | WSIHE |
| LAMP | Parents | WSIHE |
| OLDKNOW A. | Some powerful short programs | WSIHE |
| OLDKNOW A. | Some more short maths programs | WSIHE |
| OLDKNOW A., WHITE J. and CROSS J. | Conic sections | WSIHE |
| PINEL A., SHARPE R. and ELLIS R. (Eds) | Making a start | WSIHE |
| PINEL A. | Mathematical activity tile handbook | ATM |
| SMITH D. | PUMAS – Primary children understanding mathematics through microcomputer activities in schools | WSIHE |
| SMITH D. | CAMELS – Computer activities in mathematics learning strategies | WSIHE |
| TAGART C. | Small changes in my classroom | WSIHE |
| WADDINGHAM J. and WIGLEY A. (Eds) | Secondary mathematics with micros in-service pack | MEP National Mathematical Panel |

The following Open University video materials contain a significant contribution from some of the Project schools:

1. Working Mathematically with Low Attainers: Turning 'I can't' into 'I can and I did'    BBC/OU and the Mathematical Association

2. Secondary Mathematics: Classroom Practice (PM 644)    BBC/OU

In addition to all the above publications much of the material associated with the Project exists as a bank of 'working archives'. These are in the form of videos, audio tapes, personal diaries and more substantial case studies. From time to time edited selections from these will be published as articles, pamphlets and in-service resources.

Those associated with the Project continue to contribute to various courses and conferences both nationally and internationally.

# INDEX

Printed in the United Kingdom for Her Majesty's Stationery Office

Dd 8038575 12/87 C126 443 8206